686.22 BRI

W05962

D1461711

FOR
REFERENCE ONLY

ESF Design and Desktop Publishing Course

02088

Label Design 3

WOS962
(760)

LABEL DESIGN 3

THE BEST U.S. & INTERNATIONAL DESIGN

LABEL DESIGN 3

THE BEST U.S. & INTERNATIONAL DESIGN

ROCKPORT
PUBLISHERS

ART DIRECTOR: STEPHEN BRIDGES
PRODUCTION MANAGER: BARBARA STATES
BOOK DESIGN: JUDY ARISMAN/ARISMAN DESIGN
PAGE LAYOUT: JUDY ARISMAN, TONY SAIZON
TYPESETTING: PAGEMAKER 4.1
TYPOGRAPHY: HOGARTH SCRIPT/ELSNER+FLAKE
    ITC FENICE/BITSTREAM INC
OUTPUT: KRIS HILL/FINALCOPY
PRINTING: TOPPAN, SINGAPORE

Copyright © 1992 by Rockport Publishers, Inc.
All rights reserved. No part of this book may be
reproduced in any form without written
permission of the copyright owners. All images
in this book have been reproduced with the
knowledge and prior consent of the artists
concerned and no responsibility is accepted by
producer, publisher or printer for any
infringement of copyright or otherwise, arising
from the contents of this publication. Every
effort has been made to ensure that credits
accurately comply with information supplied.

First published in the United States of America by:
Rockport Publishers, Inc.
P.O. Box 396
Five Smith Street
Rockport, Massachusetts 01966
Telephone: (508) 546-9590
Fax: (508) 546-7141
Telex: 5106019284 ROCKORT PUB

Distributed to the book trade and art trade in
the U.S. and Canada by:
North Light, an imprint of
F & W Publications
1507 Dana Avenue
Cincinnati, Ohio 45207
Telephone: (513) 531-2222

Other Distribution by:
Rockport Publishers, Inc.
Rockport, Massachusetts 01966

ISBN 1-56496-005-6
10 9 8 7 6 5 4 3 2 1
Printed in Singapore

Contents

Promo and Media

AS WE MOVE CLOSER TO A GLOBAL MARKETPLACE, GRAPHICS AND SYMBOLS WILL SUPERSEDE THE

IMPORTANCE OF WORDS IN LABEL DESIGN. THE CHALLENGE FOR DESIGN FIRMS WILL BE TO UNDERSTAND

NATIONAL CULTURES IN ORDER TO MEET THE NEEDS OF THIS NEW MARKETPLACE. ✺ THIS MAY SOUND

SIMPLE IN THEORY—IN PRACTICE IT IS NOT. IT WILL REQUIRE CROSSING AN ARRAY OF CULTURAL BARRIERS

THAT HAVE BEEN IN PLACE FOR DECADES. FOR EXAMPLE, MANY BRANDS/PRODUCTS HAVE A LOYAL

CUSTOMER BASE EXCLUSIVELY IN THEIR RESPECTIVE COUNTRY OF ORIGIN, BUT ARE TOTALLY INCOMPAT-

IBLE WITH OTHER COUNTRIES/CULTURES. TO BE SUCCESSFUL, THEY MUST BE REPOSITIONED WITH THE

BRAND AS THE UNIFYING ELEMENT AND REINFORCED WITH GRAPHICS, SYMBOLS OR SEVERAL LANGUAGES

IN ORDER TO RELATE TO A GLOBAL MARKET. THE RESULT: STRONG BRANDS AND BETTER PRODUCTS

WILL GAIN THE MOST MARKET SHARE IN THIS NEW ENVIRONMENT.

Richard Gerstman and Herbert M. Meyers, Managing Partners,

Five New Stars in The Gambia

1.

1. KAIRABA
STEIGENBERGER CONSULTING/CLIENT
KNUT HARTMANN DESIGN/DESIGN FIRM
ROLAND MEHLER/ART DIRECTOR-DESIGNER-
   ILLUSTRATOR

עדיבה ממטיכה

Theadius McCall's
Jewish People!

ORIGINALS·POSTERS·PRINTS·FINE FIGURINES & COLLECTIBLES
BROOKLYN, NY · EUROPE · ISRAEL · CANADA · USA

2.

2. THEADIUS McCALL'S JEWISH PEOPLE
THEADIUS McCALL/CLIENT
ABC DESIGN STUDIO/DESIGN FIRM
ANTHONY BLOCH/ART DIRECTOR-DESIGNER

3.

3. M & CO MAILING LABELS

M & CO/DESIGN FIRM

DEAN LUBENSKY, TIBOR KALMAN/DESIGNERS

3A.

3A. M & CO MAILING LABELS

M & CO/DESIGN FIRM

STEPHEN DOYLE, TIBOR KALMAN/DESIGNERS

4. GOURMET DELI PACKAGE PROGRAM
LOUD FOOD, INC./CLIENT
SUSAN MESHBERG GRAPHIC DESIGN/DESIGN FIRM
SUSAN MESHBERG/ART DIRECTOR
SUSAN MESHBERG/DESIGNER

4.

5. LEESER FASHIONS
LEESER/CLIENT
SAMENWERKENDE ONTWERPERS BV/DESIGN FIRM
ANDRE TOET/ART DIRECTOR-DESIGNER
TJEERD FREDERIKSE/PHOTOGRAPHER

5.

6. HK SEIBU CHRISTMAS SHOPPING BAG
HONG KONG SEIBU ENTERPRISE CO LTD/CLIENT
ALAN CHAN DESIGN CO/DESIGN FIRM
ALAN CHAN/ART DIRECTOR
ALAN CHAN, PHILLIP LEUNG/DESIGNERS
GARY CHEUNG/ILLUSTRATOR

6.

7. HEICHINROU RESTAURANT

HEICHINROU RESTAURANT/CLIENT

ALAN CHAN DESIGN CO/DESIGN FIRM

ALAN CHAN, ALVIN CHAN/DESIGNERS

7.

8. DAI SEN TEA HOUSE MENU & TAKE-OUT BOX

OBUNSHA PACIFIC CORP/CLIENT

ALAN CHAN DESIGN CO/DESIGN FIRM

ALAN CHAN/ART DIRECTOR

ALAN CHAN, PHILLIP LEUNG/DESIGNERS

8.

9.

9. HK SEIBU CHRISTMAS SHOPPING BAGS
HONG KONG SEIBU ENTERPRISE CO LTD/CLIENT
ALAN CHAN DESIGN CO/DESIGN FIRM
ALAN CHAN/ART DIRECTOR
ALAN CHAN, PHILLIP LEUNG/DESIGNERS
GARY CHEUNG/ILLUSTRATOR

M&CO. 50 WEST 17 STREET NEW YORK NEW YORK 10011

YOU'RE THE TOP, YOU'RE MAHATMA GHANDI, YOU'RE THE TOP.

YOU'RE NAPOLEON BRANDY, YOU'RE THE PURPLE LIGHT OF A

SUMMER NIGHT IN SPAIN, YOU'RE THE NATIONAL GALLERY,

YOU'RE GARBO'S SALARY, YOU'RE CELLOPHANE. – C. PORTER

10.

Once upon un tempo there was a young man from Vallelunga Bel-Verde named Cicco Petrillo. He was so depressed. Perchè? Because he had no ragazza. One day while drinking espresso at Bar Lux he saw an old signora named Grattula-Bedattula who was crying. Perchè? Because her beautiful daughter Rosmarina had been kidnapped by the mean and ugly Strega Bistrega and was being held captive in the dark and impenetrable bosco. "If you can rescue her, Cicco Petrillo, she will be yours. Take this marble rock, golden scissors, and fancy paper which will insure your safety." So he set off on his quest. Suddenly a terribly large serpente lunged out from behind a bush. Cicco hurled the rock striking the bestia right on the noggin. Morte! Finito! Cicco Petrillo continued on his way until he found himself tangled in an ugly batch of brambles. Snipping furiously with the golden scissors, he set himself free. Then, as if in a dream, he heard the voice of a young damsel singing a lovely air. His cuore lept and he ran to see her. Even from

M&Co. 50 West 17 Street New York, NY 10011

10A.

11. ITALIA RESTAURANT BAGS

ITALIA/CLIENT

HORNALL ANDERSON DESIGN WORKS/DESIGN FIRM

JACK ANDERSON/ART DIRECTOR

JACK ANDERSON, JULIA LAPINE/DESIGNERS

JULIA LAPINE/ILLUSTRATOR

11.

12.

13.

13. DICRO SAMPLE PACK

PROMOTIONAL LITERATURE

OCLI (OPTICAL COATINGS LTD)/CLIENT

GRAPHIC PARTNERS/DESIGN FIRM

KEN CRAIG/ART DIRECTOR

GEOFF NICOL/DESIGNER

MICHAEL BANKS/PHOTOGRAPHER

14.

14. HOGAN'S MARKET

PUGET SOUND MARKETING CORPORATION/CLIENT

HORNALL ANDERSON DESIGN WORKS/DESIGN FIRM

JACK ANDERSON, JULIA LAPINE/ART DIRECTORS

JULIA LAPINE, DENISE WEIR, LIAN NG/DESIGNERS

LARRY JOST/ILLUSTRATOR

NANCY STENZ/HAND LETTERING

15. MONS & MERVEILLES

PAUL DECAMPS/CLIENT

B.E.P. DESIGN GROUP/DESIGN FIRM

JEAN-JACQUES EVRARD/ART DIRECTOR

CAROLE PURNELLE/DESIGNER

15.

PROMO/MEDIA

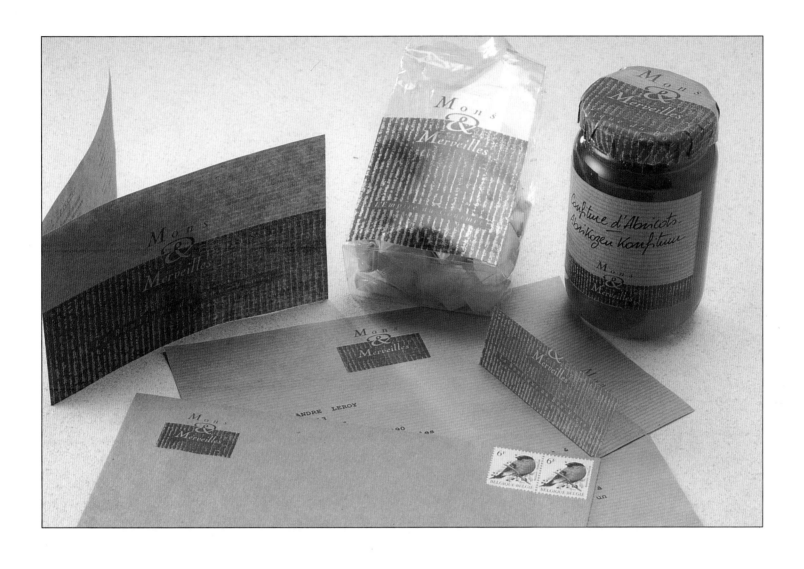

16. TACO BELL SQUEEZE BOTTLES

TACO BELL CORP/CLIENT

LIPSON-ALPORT-GLASS & ASSOC/DESIGN FIRM

17.

17. SELF-PROMO BRANDIED CHESTNUTS
BUSHA, BOSTON/DESIGN FIRM
BUSHA HUSAK/ART DIRECTOR-DESIGNER
BARRY ARRONSON/PHOTOGRAPHER

18.

18. M & CO MAILING LABEL
M & CO/DESIGN FIRM
CAROL BOKUNIEWICZ, TIBOR KALMAN/DESIGNERS

19. NETWORK APPLICATION SUPPORT
PROMOTIONAL GIFT
DIGITAL EQUIPMENT CORPORATION/CLIENT
B.E.P. DESIGN GROUP/DESIGN FIRM
JEAN-JACQUES EVRARD/ART DIRECTOR
CAROLE PURNELLE/DESIGNER-ILLUSTRATOR

19.

20. ECRU BOXES

21. ECRU PACKAGE DESIGN

ECRU/CLIENT

MARGO CHASE DESIGN/DESIGN FIRM

MARGO CHASE/ART DIRECTOR-DESIGNER

20.

21.

22. SELF-PROMO HOLIDAY JAM JAR
WALLACE CHURCH ASSOC INC/DESIGN FIRM
STANLEY CHURCH, ROBERT WALLACE/
 ART DIRECTORS
STANLEY CHURCH/DESIGNER
MARILYN MONTGOMERY/ILLUSTRATOR

22.

23. STEAMER'S SEAFOOD CAFE PACKAGING
CONSOLIDATED RESTAURANTS/CLIENT
HORNALL ANDERSON DESIGN WORKS/DESIGN FIRM
JACK ANDERSON/ART DIRECTOR
JACK ANDERSON, MARY HERMES, DAVID BATES/
 DESIGNERS
JACK ANDERSON, MARY HERMES/ILLUSTRATORS

23.

24.

24. RUMBA PRODUCT PACKAGING
WALL DATA/CLIENT
TIM GIRVIN DESIGN INC/DESIGN FIRM
TIM GIRVIN/ART DIRECTOR-ILLUSTRATOR
STEPHEN PANNONE/DESIGNER

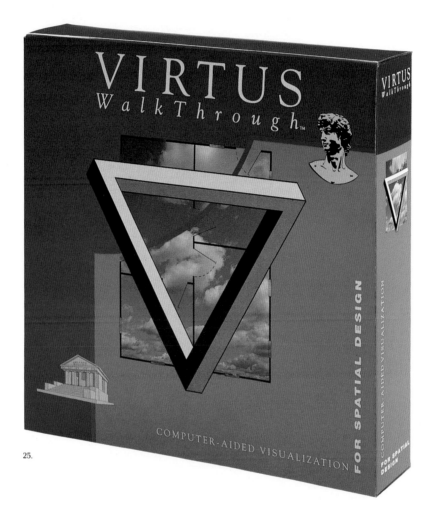

25.

25. VIRTUS WALK THROUGH
VIRTUS CORP/CLIENT
SALLY JOHNS DESIGN STUDIO/DESIGN FIRM
SALLY JOHNS/CREATIVE DIRECTOR
JEFF DALE/DESIGNER
JEFF DALE, DAVID SMITH, CHARLES FLOYD/
 ILLUSTRATORS
PICTURESQUE, F. STEVE WEBER/PHOTOGRAPHY

26. ASYMETRIX TOOLBOOK PACKAGING

ASYMETRIX CORP/CLIENT

HORNALL ANDERSON DESIGN WORKS/DESIGN FIRM

JACK ANDERSON/ART DIRECTOR

JACK ANDERSON, JULIE TANAGI-LOCK, DENISE WEIR/

  DESIGNERS

ROD AMBROSEN/ILLUSTRATOR

26.

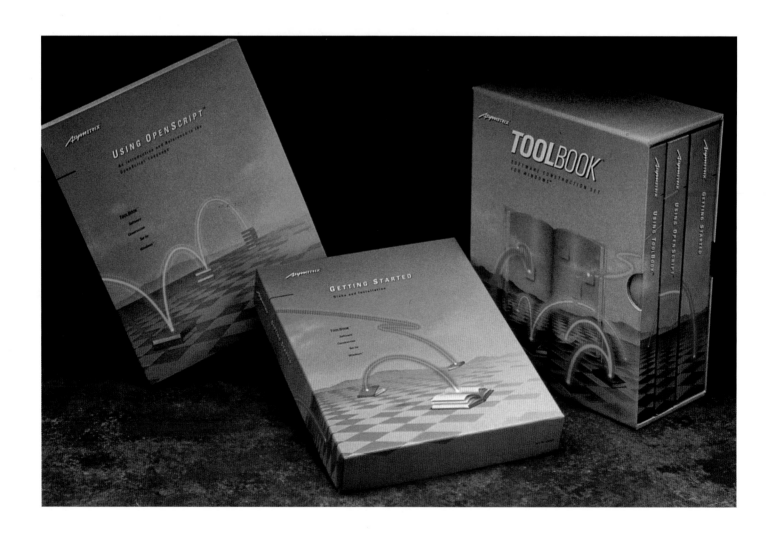

27. HOTLINE PACKAGING
GENERAL INFORMATION/CLIENT
HORNALL ANDERSON DESIGN WORKS/DESIGN FIRM
JACK ANDERSON, JULIA LAPINE/ART DIRECTORS
JACK ANDERSON, JULIA LAPINE, BRIAN O'NEILL/
 DESIGNERS
HORNALL ANDERSON/ILLUSTRATOR

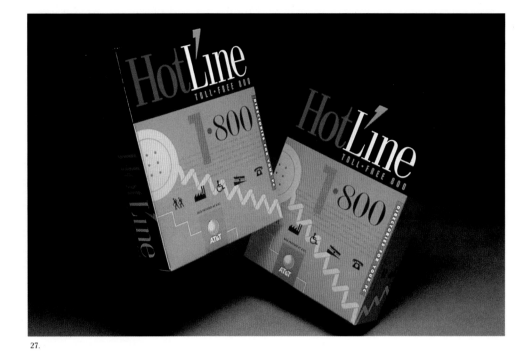

27.

28. GRAPHICAL USER INTERFACE
ASYMETRIX CORP/CLIENT
HORNALL ANDERSON DESIGN WORKS/DESIGN FIRM
JACK ANDERSON/ART DIRECTOR
JACK ANDERSON, JULIE TANAGI-LOCK, MARY HERMES,
 LIAN NG/DESIGNERS
LIAN NG/ILLUSTRATOR

28.

29. TRI-YOGA VIDEO SLEEVE

KALI RAY & MERCURY MAX/CLIENT

THARP DID IT/DESIGN FIRM

RICK THARP/ART DIRECTOR

KIM TOMLINSON, RICK THARP/DESIGNERS

PAUL SCHRAUB/PHOTOGRAPHER

29.

30. WEYERHAEUSER PULP BOXES

WEYERHAEUSER CORP/CLIENT

BELYEA DESIGN/DESIGN FIRM

JIM MCPHERSON/ART DIRECTOR

PATRICIA BELYEA/DESIGNER

GARY JACOBSEN/ILLUSTRATOR

30.

31. MACTRAC & AMTRAC/TRACKBALL PACKAGES
MICROSPEED/CLIENT
JAMIE DAVISON DESIGN INC/DESIGN FIRM
JAMIE DAVISON/ART DIRECTOR-DESIGNER

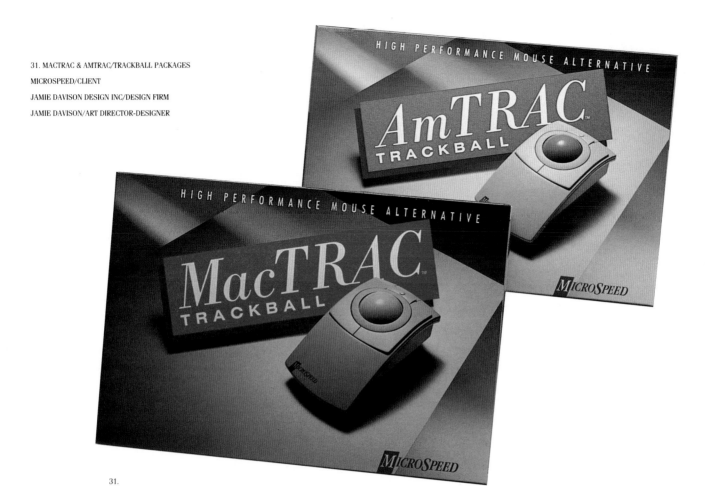

31.

32. PAINTBRUSH SERIES
ZSOFT CORPORATION/CLIENT
NEUMEIER DESIGN TEAM/DESIGN FIRM
MARTY NEUMEIER/ART DIRECTOR
CHRISTOPHER CHU, CURTIS WONG/DESIGNERS
JEANNE CARLEY, BARRIE SCHWORTZ/
 PHOTOGRAPHERS

32.

33.

33. MICROTRAC/MINIATURE TRACKBALL

MICROSPEED/CLIENT

JAMIE DAVISON DESIGN INC/DESIGN FIRM

JAMIE DAVSION/ART DIRECTOR

JAMIE DAVISON, RHONDA KIM/DESIGNERS

34.

34. THE NATURAL FOODS EDUCATION PROGRAM

BASTYR COLLEGE/CLIENT

ASCENT COMMUNICATIONS/DESIGN FIRM

ALLEN HAEGER/ART DIRECTOR-DESIGNER

DARREL TANK/ILLUSTRATOR

35.

35. "FOR DADS ONLY" VIDEO SLEEVE

LUXOR FILMS/CLIENT

ASCENT COMMUNICATIONS/DESIGN FIRM

ALLEN HAEGER/ART DIRECTOR-DESIGNER

LARRY STANLEY/PHOTOGRAPHER

PRIOR TO ESTABLISHING OUR DESIGN OFFICE, COLEMAN, LIPUMA, SEGAL & MORRILL, INC, (CLS&M) IN 1966,

o

I WORKED AS AN ACCOUNT DESIGN MANAGER FOR IRVING WERBIN ASSOCIATES. IRV PRIDED HIMSELF ON

HAVING HIS CLIENTS WITHIN ONE-QUARTER MILE OF HIS NEW YORK OFFICE. IRV WASN'T THRILLED WHEN

I VENTURED ACROSS THE PERILOUS HUDSON RIVER TO FIND DESIGN WORK IN NEW JERSEY. MY EXCURSION

INTO THE NEW WORLD RESULTED IN INCREASING IRV'S BUSINESS BY 50% WITHIN THE FIRST YEAR. ≈ IRV

RECENTLY RETURNED FROM THE ROTHSCHILD CHATEAU AND SPOKE OF THE MERITS OF WORKING FOR

CLIENTS IN DISTANT PLACES. ≈ UPON VISITING CLS&M'S DESIGN OFFICE, HE WITNESSED OUR COMPUTER

REMOTE TRANSMISSION OF DESIGN CONCEPTS TO OUR CLIENTS IN THE UNITED STATES AND EUROPE.

VISUAL ANNOTATIONS WERE MADE IN "REAL TIME," WITH MODEST CHANGES SENT BACK TO THE CLIENTS

WITHIN A FEW HOURS. IRV WAS PROUD THAT I FINALLY CAME AROUND TO HIS WAY OF THINKING: I COULD

NOW STAY IN MY OFFICE AND WORK WITH CLIENTS WITHIN A QUARTER MILE RADIUS—OR BEYOND

≈ I GUESS NOT MUCH HAS CHANGED OVER THE LAST THIRTY YEARS.

Owen W. Coleman, President
Coleman, Lipuma, Segal & Morrill Inc

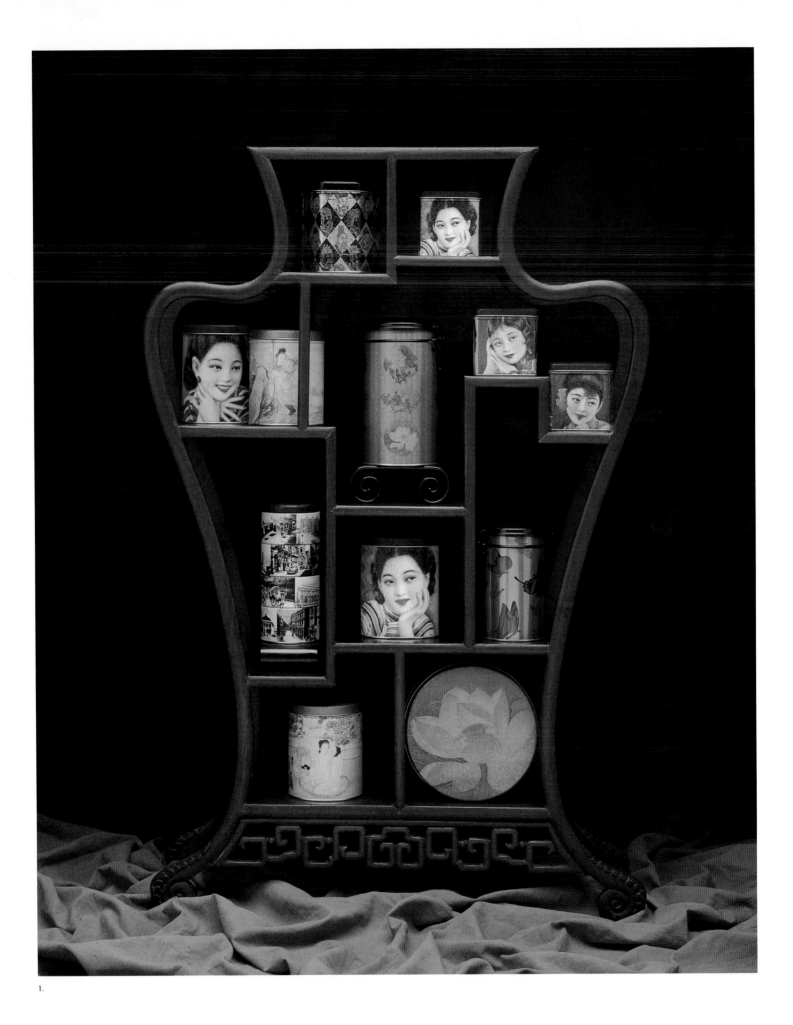

1.

CONSUMER

1. DAI SEN TEA HOUSE TINS
OBUNSHA PACIFIC CORP/CLIENT
ALAN CHAN DESIGN CO/DESIGN FIRM
ALAN CHAN/ART DIRECTOR
ALAN CHAN, PHILLIP LEUNG/DESIGNERS

2. ART OF LIVING
DORMA/CLIENT
TRICKETT & WEBB/DESIGN FIRM
LYNN TRICKETT, BRIAN WEBB,
 AVRIL BROADLEY/ DESIGNERS
TRICKETT & WEBB/ILLUSTRATOR

2.

3. DAI SEN TEA HOUSE TINS

OBUNSHA PACIFIC CORP/CLIENT

ALAN CHAN DESIGN CO/DESIGN FIRM

ALAN CHAN/ART DIRECTOR

ALAN CHAN, PHILLIP LEUNG/DESIGNERS

3.

4. ILLUMINATED GLOBE
W.H. SMITH/CLIENT
TRICKETT & WEBB/DESIGN FIRM
BRIAN WEBB, LYNN TRICKETT,
 SUZANNE EVANS/DESIGNERS
PETER MARSHALL/PHOTOGRAPHER

4.

5. MAXELL VIDEOCASSETTES
MAXELL CORP OF AMERICA/CLIENT
GERSTMAN+MEYERS INC/DESIGN FIRM
HERBERT M. MEYERS/OVERALL SUPERVISOR
JUAN CONCEPCION/CREATIVE DIRECTOR
SABRA WAXMAN/DESIGN DIRECTOR
JOHN WASKI/DESIGNER

5.

7. JOCKEY'S MENS CLASSIC BRIEFS
JOCKEY INTERNATIONAL/CLIENT
GRAPHIC PARTNERS/DESIGN FIRM
GRAHAM DUFFY/ART DIRECTOR-DESIGNER
SANDY PORTER/PHOTOGRAPHER

6.

6. COPENHAGEN
US TOBACCO INC/CLIENT
THE BERNI COMPANY/DESIGN FIRM
MARK ECKSTEIN/ART DIRECTOR
PETER ANTIPAS/DESIGNER

7.

8. GIANNA CO LTD POTPOURRI

GIANNA CO LTD/CLIENT

ALAN CHAN DESIGN CO/DESIGN FIRM

ALAN CHAN/ART DIRECTOR

ALAN CHAN, ANDY YIP/DESIGNERS

8.

10. K2 SKIS
K2 CORP/CLIENT
HORNALL ANDERSON DESIGN WORKS/
 DESIGN FIRM
JACK ANDERSON/ART DIRECTOR
JACK ANDERSON, JANI DREWFS, DAVID BATES/
 DESIGNERS

9. K2 GOGGLE PACKAGING
K2 CORP/CLIENT
HORNALL ANDERSON DESIGN WORKS/
 DESIGN FIRM
JACK ANDERSON/ART DIRECTOR
JACK ANDERSON, DAVID BATES, MIKE COURTNEY/
 DESIGNERS

9.

10. K2 SKIS

CONSUMER

10.

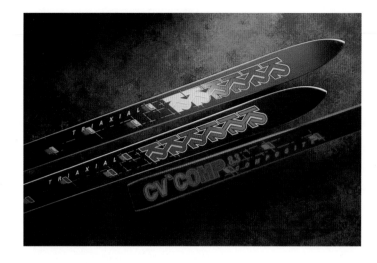

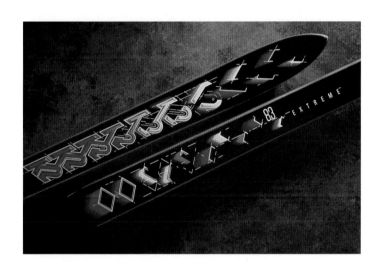

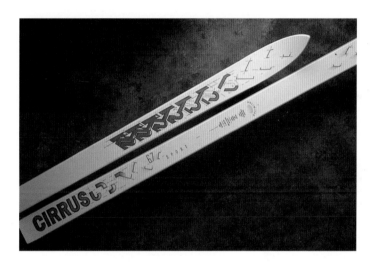

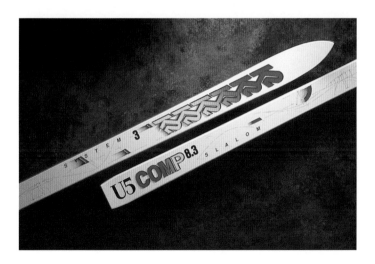

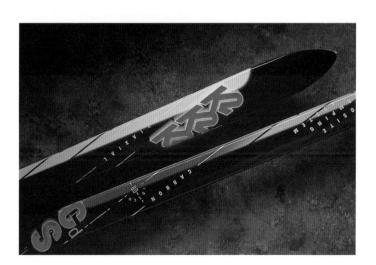

11.

CONSUMER

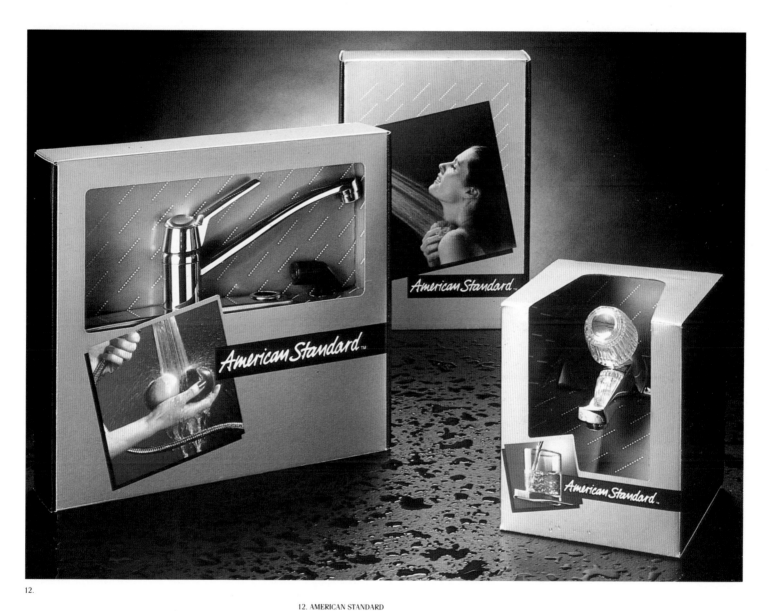

12.

13. NEWPORT HARBOR MENSWEAR

WHALING INDUSTRIES/CLIENT

THE DESIGN COMPANY/DESIGN FIRM

MARCIA ROMANUCK/ART DIRECTOR-DESIGNER

CHESAPEAKE STUDIOS/PHOTOGRAPHER

13.

14.

14. CALDOR PRIVATE LABEL HANG TAGS
CALDOR INC/CLIENT
THE BERNI COMPANY/DESIGN FIRM
STUART M. BERNI/ART DIRECTOR
MARK ECKSTEIN/DESIGNER

15. TILE SAMPLE BOX

DELEO CLAY TILE/CLIENT

MIRES DESIGN/DESIGN FIRM

JOSE SERRANO/ART DIRECTOR, DESIGNER

TRACY SABIN/ILLUSTRATOR

15.

16. COFFEE BUTLER SUPER 50

THE THERMOS CO/CLIENT

LIPSON-ALPORT-GLASS & ASSOC/DESIGN FIRM

16.

17.

17. HOLIDAY COLLECTION

SHAKLEE/CLIENT

JAMIE DAVISON DESIGN INC/DESIGN FIRM

JAMIE DAVISON/ART DIRECTOR

JAMIE DAVISON, JEANETTE BRYSKIER,

RHONDA KIM/DESIGNERS

18. AMAZON SMYTHE PET FOODS

KAYTEE PRODUCTS INC/CLIENT

MURRIE, WHITE, DRUMMOND, LIENHART/
 DESIGN FIRM

WAYNE KRIMSTON, JOE BRUCATO/ART DIRECTORS-
 DESIGNERS

DON TATE/ILLUSTRATOR

PAUL RUNG/PHOTOGRAPHER

18.

19. KAYTEE WILD BIRD FOOD

KAYTEE PRODUCTS INC/CLIENT

MURRIE, WHITE, DRUMMOND, LIENHART/
 DESIGN FIRM

JEFF WHITE/ART DIRECTOR-DESIGNER

DON TATE/ILLUSTRATOR

19.

20.

20. KAYTEE MORE BIRD TREATS
KAYTEE PRODUCTS INC/CLIENT
MURRIE, WHITE, DRUMMOND, LIENHART/
 DESIGN FIRM
LINDA VOLL/ART DIRECTOR-DESIGNER
DON TATE/ILLUSTRATOR
PAUL RUNG/PHOTOGRAPHER

21. GRAND UNION BIRD FOOD
THE GRAND UNION COMPANY/CLIENT
MILTON GLASER INC/DESIGN FIRM
MILTON GLASER, DAVID FREEDMAN/
 ART DIRECTORS
CHI-MING KAN/DESIGNER-ILLUSTRATOR

21.

CONSUMER

22.

22. PUPPIZZA DOG TREATS

BEST BRED PRODUCTS/CLIENT

LIPSON-ALPORT-GLASS & ASSOC/DESIGN FIRM

23. ART OF LIVING
DORMA/CLIENT
TRICKETT & WEBB/DESIGN FIRM
LYNN TRICKETT, BRIAN WEBB,
AVRIL BROADLEY/ DESIGNERS
TRICKETT & WEBB/ILLUSTRATOR

23.

STRAWBERRY HILL

A UNIQUE NEW COLLECTION

OF DORMA CO-ORDINATED HOME

FURNISHINGS, WITH THE

ACCENT ON STYLE, AND THE

DORMA GUARANTEE OF QUALITY.

WEDGEWOOD

FLAME STRIPE

A UNIQUE NEW COLLECTION

OF DORMA CO-ORDINATED HOME

FURNISHINGS, WITH THE

ACCENT ON STYLE, AND THE

DORMA GUARANTEE OF QUALITY.

MULBERRY / NAVY

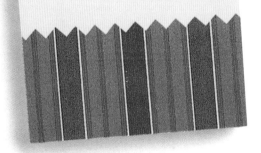

24. CATFLAP

ANTHONY GREEN PET PRODUCTS/CLIENT

TRICKETT & WEBB/DESIGN FIRM

BRIAN WEBB, LYNN TRICKETT, IAN COCKBURN/
  DESIGNERS

TRICKETT & WEBB/ILLUSTRATOR

24.

25. WHISKER LICKINS CAT TREATS

RALSTON PURINA/CLIENT

KULLBERG-JOHNSON ASSOC/DESIGN FIRM

PENNY JOHNSON/ART DIRECTOR-DESIGNER

25.

26. BASTED DOG TREATS

HARPER LEATHER GOODS MFG CO/CLIENT

MURRIE, WHITE, DRUMMOND, LIENHART/
  DESIGN FIRM

JAYCE DOUGALL SCHMIDT/ART DIRECTOR-
  DESIGNER

26.

27.

27. FRISKIES

NESTLE-FRISKIES PETCARE PRODUCTS/CLIENT

COLEMAN, LIPUMA, SEGAL & MORRILL/DESIGN FIRM

OWEN COLEMAN, JOHN CHRZANOWSKI/
 ART DIRECTORS

WILLIAM LEE, LORRAINE FIERRO, CATHERINE SZE-TU/
 DESIGNERS

HENRY BJON STUDIO/PHOTOGRAPHER

28.

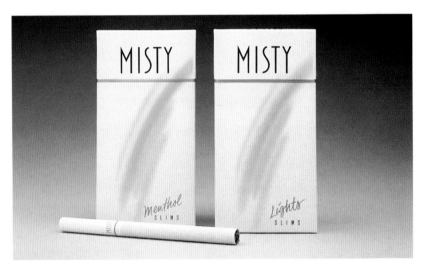

28A.

28B.

28. MONTCLAIR

THE AMERICAN TOBACCO COMPANY/CLIENT

PETERSON & BLYTH ASSOCIATES/DESIGN FIRM

RONALD PETERSON/ART DIRECTOR

BOB CRUANAS/DESIGNER

28A. MISTY

THE AMERICAN TOBACCO COMPANY/CLIENT

PETERSON & BLYTH ASSOCIATES/DESIGN FIRM

JOHN BLYTH/ART DIRECTOR

BOB CRUANAS/DESIGNER

28B. MALIBU

THE AMERICAN TOBACCO COMPANY/CLIENT

PETERSON & BLYTH ASSOCIATES/DESIGN FIRM

JOHN BLYTH/ART DIRECTOR

BOB CRUANAS/DESIGNER

CONSUMER

29.

29. SELECT

US TOBACCO INC/CLIENT

THE BERNI COMPANY/DESIGN FIRM

MARK ECKSTEIN/ART DIRECTOR

PETER ANTIPAS/DESIGNER

30.

30. FORUM CIGARETTES

POTOMAC INC/CLIENT

VARDIMON DESIGN/DESIGN FIRM

YAROM VARDIMON/ART DIRECTOR-DESIGNER-

 ILLUSTRATOR

31. MICKEY'S WAFFLER

VITANTONIO MANUFACTURING COMPANY/CLIENT

ADE SKUNTA AND CO/DESIGN FIRM

KAREN A. SKUNTA/ART DIRECTOR-DESIGNER

32.

32. FREEZLOC

DOWBRANDS/CLIENT

PACKAGE DESIGN OF AMERICA/DESIGN FIRM

ALAN ANDERSON, GARY HOLD/DESIGNERS

HUGH HURTLE/ILLUSTRATOR

33.

33. KETER COCKTAIL GLASSES

KETER PLASTIC LTD/CLIENT

STUDIO KALDERON/DESIGN FIRM

ASHER KALDERON/ART DIRECTOR-DESIGNER

ITAMAR/PHOTOGRAPHER

34. TURBO 1-2-3 SOAP

BRAVOPACK/CLIENT

YESTRA GRAPHIC DESIGN/DESIGN FIRM

MARTEN YESTRA, AAD VAN LUYK/ART

 DIRECTORS

MARTEN YESTRA/DESIGNER-ILLUSTRATOR

34.

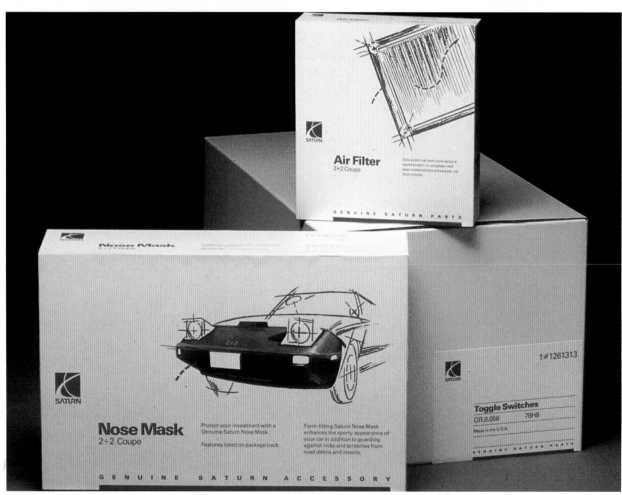

35.

35. SATURN PACKAGING

GM SATURN/CLIENT

DESIGN FORUM/DESIGN FIRM

RENAE ROBERTS/DESIGNER

CONSUMER

36.

36. FENWICK FLYLINES

FENWICK/CLIENT

HARTE YAMASHITA & FOREST/DESIGN FIRM

SUSAN HEALY/ART DIRECTOR-DESIGNER

37.

37. PEAK PRODUCTS

OLD WORLD AUTOMOTIVE PRODUCTS INC/CLIENT

ADVANCE DESIGN CENTER/DESIGN FIRM

JAIME SENDRA/ART DIRECTOR

BRYAN ROGERS/DESIGNER

38. CASTROL MOTOR OIL

CASTROL INC/CLIENT

COLEMAN LIPUMA SEGAL & MORRILL INC/
 DESIGN FIRM

SAL V. LIPUMA, ABE SEGAL/CREATIVE DIRECTORS

WILLIAM LEE/DESIGNER

38.

CONSUMER

39

39. SLEEK LIQUID CAR WAX
S.C. JOHNSON & SON INC/CLIENT
MURRIE, WHITE, DRUMMOND, LIENHART/
 DESIGN FIRM
AMY LEPPERT SHANNON/ART DIRECTOR-DESIGNER
PAUL RUNG/PHOTOGRAPHER

40.

40. ZEREX ANTIFREEZE COOLANT

BASF CORP/CLIENT

GERSTMAN+MEYERS INC/DESIGN FIRM

HERBERT M. MEYERS/OVERALL SUPERVISOR

JUAN CONCEPCION/CREATIVE DIRECTOR

JEFF ZACK, JUDITH MILLER/DESIGNERS

42. 3M NEW PRODUCT LINE

3M CO/CLIENT

COLEMAN LIPUMA SEGAL & MORRILL INC/
 DESIGN FIRM

OWEN W. COLEMAN, JOHN CHRZANOWSKI/
 CREATIVE DIRECTORS

JOHN SCOLLIN, JOHN CHRZANOWSKI/DESIGNERS

41.

41. SYNTEC

CASTROL INC/CLIENT

COLEMAN LIPUMA SEGAL & MORRILL INC/
 DESIGN FIRM

SAL V. LIPUMA, ABE SEGAL/CREATIVE DIRECTORS

WILLIAM LEE/DESIGNER

42.

43.

43. ECLIPSE 10 PAINT LABEL

SAXON PAINT & HOME CARE CENTER/CLIENT

PORTER, MATJASICH & ASSOC/DESIGN FIRM

ALLEN PORTER/ART DIRECTOR-DESIGNER

LISA ELLERT/ILLUSTRATOR

44. COVERCOAT PAINT LABEL

SAXON PAINT & HOME CARE CENTER/CLIENT

PORTER, MATJASICH & ASSOC/DESIGN FIRM

ALLEN PORTER/ART DIRECTOR-DESIGNER

44.

45.

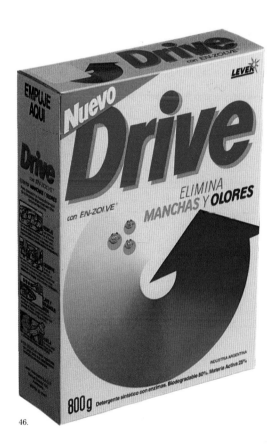

46.

45. PMC PAINT LABEL

SAXON PAINT & HOME CARE CENTERS/CLIENT

PORTER, MATJASICH & ASSOC/DESIGN FIRM

ALLEN PORTER/ART DIRECTOR

ROBERT RAUSCH/DESIGNER

MARIA STROESTER/ILLUSTRATOR

46. DRIVE POWDER DETERGENT

LEVER Y ASOCIADOS S.A.C.I.F./CLIENT

DIL CONSULTANTS IN DESIGN/DESIGN FIRM

47.

47. DOW BATHROOM CLEANER

DOWBRANDS/CLIENT

PACKAGE DESIGN OF AMERICA/DESIGN FIRM

TED GIAVIS/ILLUSTRATOR

48. MAGIC SIZING

THE DIAL CORP/CLIENT

COLEMAN LIPUMA SEGAL & MORRILL INC/

 DESIGN FIRM

OWEN W. COLEMAN, ABE SEGAL/

 CREATIVE DIRECTORS

WILLIAM LEE/DESIGNER

48.

49. COMET

PROCTOR & GAMBLE CO/CLIENT

MURRIE, WHITE, DRUMMOND, LIENHART/

 DESIGN FIRM

WAYNE KRIMSTON/ART DIRECTOR-DESIGNER

PAUL RUNG/PHOTOGRAPHER

49.

50.

50. CLEATS

REMCO/CLIENT

DESIGNED TO PRINT & ASSOC INC/DESIGN FIRM

PEGGY LEONARD, TREE TRAPANESE/
 ART DIRECTORS

PEGGY LEONARD/DESIGNER-ILLUSTRATOR

51.

51. BIC FLUO-RANGE

BIC CORP/CLIENT

B.E.P. DESIGN GROUP/DESIGN FIRM

BRIGITTE EVRARD/ART DIRECTOR

CAROLE PURNELLE/DESIGNER-ILLUSTRATOR

52. RECORD BREAKERS

HASBRO/CLIENT

DESIGNED TO PRINT & ASSOCIATES LTD/
 DESIGN FIRM

TREE TRAPANESE, PEGGY LEONARD, DAVID UN/
 ART DIRECTORS

TREE TRAPANESE, PEGGY LEONARD/DESIGNERS

52.

53.

53. BIC WAVELENGTHS

BIC CORP/CLIENT

GERSTMAN+MEYERS INC/DESIGN FIRM

RICHARD GERSTMAN/OVERALL SUPERVISOR

JUAN CONCEPCION/CREATIVE DIRECTOR

LISA KEYKO/DESIGN DIRECTOR

JEFF ZACK, MARIANNE WALTHER/DESIGNERS

54.

54. PREMIUM ROLL DOG FOOD

SHEPHERDS/CLIENT

GRAPHIC PARTNERS/DESIGN FIRM

GRAHAM DUFFY/ART DIRECTOR

OONAGH DON/DESIGNER

ALAN THOMSON/ILLUSTRATOR

55. PHILIPS LIGHTBULBS
NORTH AMERICAN PHILIPS/CLIENT
KOLLBERG-JOHNSON ASSOC/DESIGN FIRM
GARY KOLLBERG/ART DIRECTOR-DESIGNER

55.

56. ZODIAC PET PROTECTION PRODUCTS
ZOECON CORP/CLIENT
COLEMAN LIPUMA SEGAL & MORRILL INC/
 DESIGN FIRM
EDWARD MORRILL, RICHARD C. ROTH/
 CREATIVE DIRECTORS
WILLIAM LEE, LORRAINE FIERRO,
 SARAH ALLEN/DESIGNERS
J.C. CHOU/ILLUSTRATOR

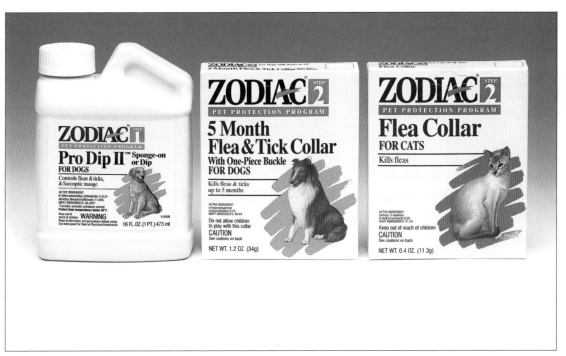

56.

Health

and

Beauty

PACKAGING IS REALLY WHAT GRAPHIC DESIGN IS ALL ABOUT. ULTIMATELY, THE GOAL AND THE PRINCIPLE

ACHIEVEMENT OF GRAPHIC DESIGN IS THE PACKAGING OF CONCEPTS. A STATIONERY SYSTEM PRESENTS

THE "PACKAGE" OF THE THINKING AND SPIRIT OF A CORPORATION. AN ANNUAL REPORT PACKAGES OR

ENCAPSULATES THE CONSCIOUSNESS AND FINANCIAL PROGRESS OF A BUSINESS. THE EXTERIOR OF A

BUILDING IS, IN FACT, A PACKAGE WHICH CONTAINS THE SPIRIT OF THE PEOPLE AND PRODUCTS WITHIN.

AND, FINALLY, A DEFTLY CREATED LOGOTYPE SUGGESTS BY ITS ARTFUL LETTERFORM, THE PACKAGING

OF AN IDEA WHICH IS ULTIMATELY DISSEMINATED TO ITS AUDIENCE. AS DESIGNERS, WE CREATE BOXES

WITHIN BOXES. THE OUTSIDE OF A STORE, IN TURN, HOLDS THE PRODUCTS WITHIN. THE PRODUCTS

WITHIN HOLD THE PRODUCT ITSELF. THUS, THE SEED OF THE IDEA AND THE SPIRIT OF A CORPORATION

OR THE QUALITY OF A PRODUCT IS THEN SUMMARIZED IN ITS PACKAGE.

Tim Girvin, Principal
Tim Girvin Design Inc

1.

HEALTH/BEAUTY

1. GARDEN BOTANIKA PRODUCTS

GARDEN BOTANIKA/CLIENT

TIM GIRVIN DESIGN INC/DESIGN FIRM

TIM GIRVIN/ART DIRECTOR

STEPHEN PANNONE/DESIGNER-ILLUSTRATOR

2. SLIM & NATURAL DIET DRINK

NATURAL ORGANICS INC/CLIENT

APPLE DESIGNSOURCE INC/DESIGN FIRM

BARRY G. SEELIG/ART DIRECTOR

NANCY P. BROGDEN, KAREN WILLOUGHBY/

 DESIGNERS

LASZLO STERN/PHOTOGRAPHER

3.

HEARTPLAN

SHAKLEE/CLIENT

JAMIE DAVISON DESIGN INC/DESIGN FIRM

JAMIE DAVISON/ART DIRECTOR

JAMIE DAVISON, JEANETTE BRYSKIER/

 DESIGNERS

2.

4 SPIRU-TEIN MEAL REPLACEMENT

NATURAL ORGANICS INC/CLIENT

APPLE DESIGNSOURCE INC/DESIGN FIRM

BARRY G. SEELIG/ART DIRECTOR

NANCY P. BROGDEN, KAREN WILLOUGHBY/

 DESIGNERS

LASZLO STERN/PHOTOGRAPHER

4.

5.

5. GOPOWER

KARVO INC/CLIENT

ASCENT COMMUNICATIONS/DESIGN FIRM

ALLEN HAEGER/ART DIRECTOR

MICHAEL LATIL/PHOTOGRAPHER

6. YERBA PRIMA WEIGHT LOSS PROGRAM

YERBA PRIMA/CLIENT

ASCENT COMMUNICATIONS/DESIGN FIRM

ALLEN HAEGER/ART DIRECTOR

ROGER GEFVERT/ILLUSTRATOR

6.

7. VERVE PARFUME DEODORANT

CHESEBROUGH-PONDS ITALY/CLIENT

KOLLBERG-JOHNSON ASSOC/DESIGN FIRM

PENNY JOHNSON/ART DIRECTOR-DESIGNER

7.

8. RAVE HAIR PRODUCTS
CHESEBROUGH-PONDS USA/CLIENT
THE BERNI COMPANY/DESIGN FIRM
MARK ECKSTEIN/ART DIRECTOR
PAUL BELUK/DESIGNER

8.

9. H20 HEALTHCARE PRODUCTS

J.M. HOLDINGS/CLIENT

MURRIE, WHITE, DRUMMOND, LIENHART/

  DESIGN FIRM

JAMES LIENHART/ART DIRECTOR-DESIGNER

PAUL RUNG/PHOTOGRAPHER

9.

10.

10. KISS MY FACE MOISTURE BATH

KISS MY FACE/CLIENT

ALTERNATIVES/DESIGN FIRM

JULIE KOCH-BEINKE/ART DIRECTOR

KEVIN YATES/DESIGNER-PHOTOGRAPHER

11. KASHMIR

PIER 1 IMPORTS/CLIENT

THE JOPPA GROUP/DESIGN FIRM

BRUCE DEMUSTCHINE/ART DIRECTOR

IRENE JOHNSON/DESIGNER

ELIZABETH GOLZ RUSH/ILLUSTRATOR

11.

HEALTH/BEAUTY

12. BAN ANTI-PERSPIRANT DEODORANT

BRISTOL-MEYERS SQUIBB CO/CLIENT

MURRIE, WHITE, DRUMMOND, LIENHART/

 DESIGN FIRM

KATE MCSHERRY/ART DIRECTOR-DESIGNER

12.

13. SABOR E FORCA VITAMIN POWDER

FLEISCHMANN E ROYAL MILK PRODUCTS/CLIENT

DIL CONSULTANTS IN DESIGN/DESIGN FIRM

DIL DESIGN TEAM/ART DIRECTORS

13.

14. LISTERINE ANTISEPTIC

WARNER-LAMBERT CO/CLIENT

GERSTMAN+MEYERS INC/DESIGN FIRM

RICHARD GERSTMAN/OVERALL SUPERVISOR

JUAN CONCEPCION/CREATIVE DIRECTOR

JEFF ZACK, JUDITH MILLER/DESIGNERS

RIC HIRST, RICHARD EDSTROM/STRUCTURAL DESIGNERS

14.

15.

15. KISS MY FACE GLYCERINE MOISTURE SOAP

KISS MY FACE/CLIENT

ALTERNATIVES/DESIGN FIRM

JULIE KOCH-BEINKE/ART DIRECTOR

LYNN SCHERER/DESIGNER

16. H20 HEALTHCARE PRODUCTS

J.M. HOLDINGS/CLIENT

MURRIE, WHITE, DRUMMOND, LIENHART/
 DESIGN FIRM

JAMES LIENHART/ART DIRECTOR-DESIGNER

PAUL RUNG/PHOTOGRAPHER

16.

17. CHILDREN'S NYQUIL

RICHARDSON VICKS INC/CLIENT

HANS FLINK DESIGN INC/DESIGN FIRM

HANS D. FLINK/ART DIRECTOR

HANS D. FLINK, JANE PARASZCZAK/DESIGNERS

JAQUE AUGER/ILLUSTRATOR

17.

18. AMERICE HAND SOAPS
MARSHALL FIELD'S/CLIENT
MURRIE, WHITE, DRUMMOND, LIENHART/
 DESIGN FIRM
LINDA VOLL/ART DIRECTOR-DESIGNER-
 ILLUSTRATOR
PAUL RUNG/PHOTOGRAPHER

18.

19. EXCEDRIN PM LIQUID
BRISTOL-MEYERS SQUIBB CO/CLIENT
MURRIE, WHITE, DRUMMOND, LIENHART/
 DESIGN FIRM
DALE FAHNSTROM/ART DIRECTOR-DESIGNER
PAUL RUNG/PHOTOGRAPHER

19.

20. MAUA VERT PERFUMES

PERFUMES MAUA LTDA/CLIENT

DIL CONSULTANTS IN DESIGN/DESIGN FIRM

DIL DESIGN TEAM/ART DIRECTORS

21. KISS OFF

KISS MY FACE/CLIENT

ALTERNATIVES/DESIGN FIRM

JULIE KOCH-BEINKE/ART DIRECTOR

LYNN SCHERER/DESIGNER

20.

21.

22. A.C.T. SWIMMERS SHAMPOO
DENA CORPORATION/CLIENT
MURRIE, WHITE, DRUMMOND, LIENHART/
 DESIGN FIRM
WAYNE KRIMSTON/ART DIRECTOR-DESIGNER
DON TATE/ILLUSTRATOR

22.

23. CLEAR BY DESIGN
SMITHKLINE BEECHAM/CLIENT
GERSTMAN+MEYERS INC/DESIGN FIRM
HERBERT M. MEYERS INC/OVERALL SUPERVISOR
JUAN CONCEPCION/CREATIVE SUPERVISOR
LISA KEYKO/DESIGN DIRECTOR
JOE LOMBARDO/DESIGNER

23.

24. ULTRA DIET QUICK

TKI INC/CLIENT

PACKAGE DESIGN OF AMERICA/DESIGN FIRM

ALAN ANDERSON, GARY HOLDA/DESIGNERS

ELEANOR THOMPSON/PHOTOGRAPHER

24.

25. JOHN FRIEDA HAIR CARE PRODUCTS

JOHN FRIEDA/CLIENT

TRICKETT & WEBB/DESIGN FIRM

BRIAN WEBB, LYNN TRICKETT, FIONA SKELSEY/

 DESIGNERS

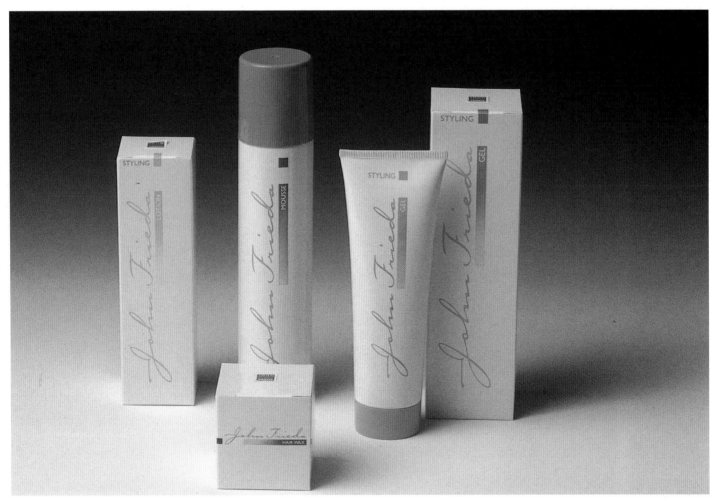

25.

HEALTH/BEAUTY

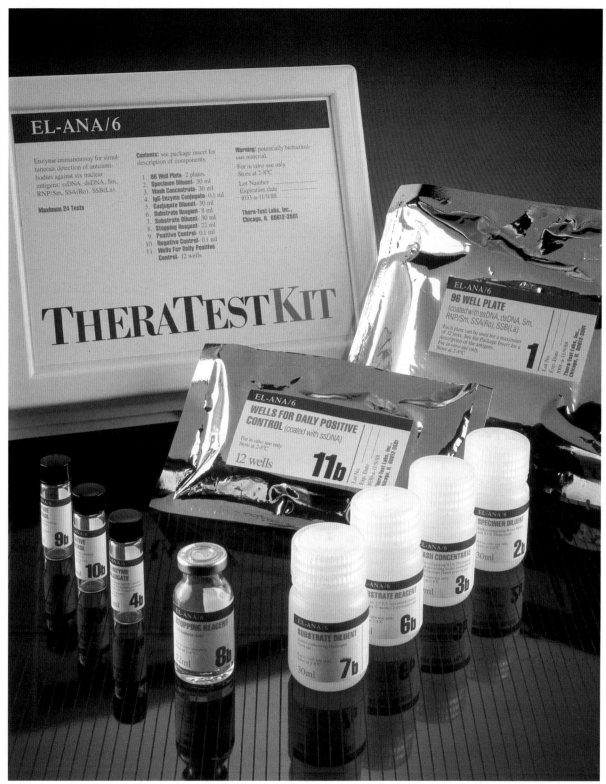

26.

26. THERATEST

THERATEST LABS/CLIENT

MICHAEL STANARD INC./DESIGN FIRM

MICHAEL STANARD/ART DIRECTOR

MARCOS CHAVEZ/DESIGNER

27. GELINAS

GELINAS/CLIENT

MARGO CHASE DESIGN/DESIGN FIRM

MARGO CHASE/ART DIRECTOR-DESIGNER

MINDAS/PHOTOGRAPHER

27.

HEALTH/BEAUTY

28. GAVISCON

MARION LABORATORIES/CLIENT

GERSTMAN+MEYERS INC/DESIGN FIRM

HERBERT M. MEYERS/OVERALL SUPERVISOR

JUAN CONCEPCION/CREATIVE SUPERVISOR

KAREN CORELL, ROBIN KUPFER, RICHARD EDSTROM/

DESIGNERS

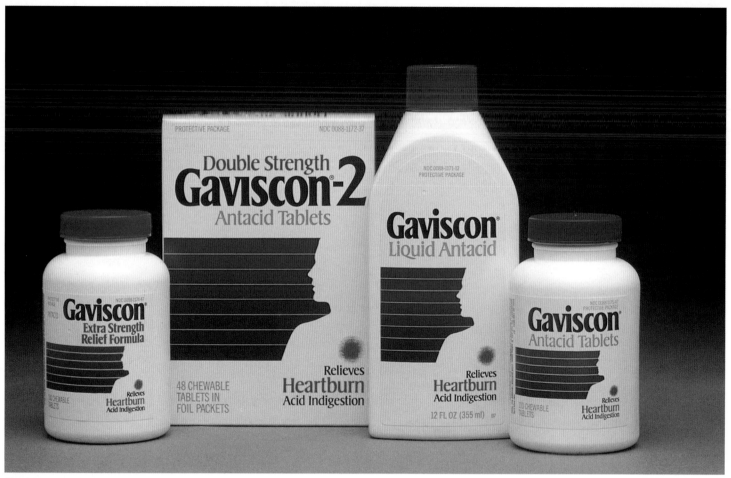

28.

28A. STAYFREE

PERSONAL PRODUCTS CO/CLIENT

GERSTMAN+MEYERS INC/DESIGN FIRM

RICHARD GERSTMAN/OVERALL SUPERVISOR

JUAN CONCEPCION/CREATIVE SUPERVISOR

RAFAEL FELICIANO/DESIGN DIRECTOR

MARIANNE WALTHER/DESIGNER

28A.

29. PERSONAL CARE PRODUCTS FOR CHILDREN
WILLIAM & CLARISSA/CLIENT
COGNATA & ASSOC/DESIGN FIRM
RICHARD COGNATA/ART DIRECTOR-DESIGNER

29.

30. VASELINE INTENSIVE CARE LINE
CHESEBROUGH-PONDS USA/CLIENT
HANS FLINK DESIGN INC/DESIGN FIRM
HANS D. FLINK/ART DIRECTOR
HANS D. FLINK, JANE PARASZCZAK/DESIGNERS

30.

31.

31. LA LOOKS MAKE-UP KIT
DEP CORPORATION/CLIENT
SHIMOKOCHI-REEVES DESIGN/DESIGN FIRM
MAMORU SHIMOKOCHI, ANNE REEVES/ART
 DIRECTORS
MAMORU SHIMOKOCHI, ANNE REEVES,
TRACY MCGOLDRICK/DESIGNERS

32.

32. LA LOOKS HAIR STYLING PRODUCTS
DEP CORPORATION/CLIENT
SHIMOKOCHI-REEVES DESIGN/DESIGN FIRM
MAMORU SHIMOKOCHI, ANNE REEVES/ART
 DIRECTORS-DESIGNERS

33. CARESS GLYCERINE TOILET SOAP
IND. GESSY LEVER LTDA - UNILEVER/CLIENT
DIL CONSULTANTS IN DESIGN/DESIGN FIRM
DIL DESIGN TEAM/ART DIRECTORS

33.

34. PANTENE HAIRBRUSH LINE
RICHARDSON VICKS INC/CLIENT
HANS FLINK DESIGN INC/DESIGN FIRM
HANS D. FLINK/ART DIRECTOR
JANE PARASZCZAK, HANS D. FLINK/DESIGNERS

34.

HEALTH/BEAUTY

35. MENS GIFTS

PRINTED TINS AND CARD BOOKS

BOOTS/CLIENT

TRICKETT & WEBB/DESIGN FIRM

BRIAN WEBB, LYNN TRICKETT, ANDREW THOMAS/
 DESIGNERS

PAUL LEITH, MARK THOMAS, TONY MCSWEENEY/
 ILLUSTRATORS

Beer

and

Liquor

AS THE WORLD MARKET SHRINKS TO SEVERAL LARGE GLOBAL AREAS, THERE IS A GROWING DANGER

THAT PACKAGING WILL BECOME INCREASINGLY BLAND. YET "PAN EUROPEAN" COULD HAVE AS MUCH

INTEREST AS IT'S ELDERLY COUSIN "PAN AMERICAN" GRAPHICS, IF ENCOURAGED TO PROLIFERATE. ❧ THE

VERY NATURE OF THE PRODUCTS FROM SMALLER AREAS OR COUNTRIES, MAKES THEM UNIQUE AND

INTERESTING. ENCOURAGED BY THEIR COMPACT MARKETS WITH FACTORY-TO-STORE-IN-ONE-DAY

DISTRIBUTION NETWORKS, REGIONAL OR NICHE PRODUCTS FLOURISH. LITTLE WONDER THAT BRITISH

PACKAGING DESIGN CONTINUES TO DOMINATE THE MAJOR INTERNATIONAL AWARDS. ❧ FAR BETTER FOR

THEM TO GROW INTO INTERNATIONAL PRODUCTS FOR THESE QUALITIES THAN TO SUFFER THE DEAD

HAND OF GLOBAL LOGISTICS. ❧ PACKAGING IS ULTIMATELY JUDGED NOT BY THOSE WHO EMPLOY THE DE-

SIGNERS, BUT BY THOSE WHO BUY THE PRODUCTS. WHY TAKE THE PLEASURE OF INNOVATIVE EXCITING

PACKAGING AWAY FROM THEM?

Graphic Partners, Edinburgh

1.

BEER / LIQUOR

1. PAT O'BRIEN'S HURRICANE

HEUBLEIN INC/CLIENT

KLIM DESIGN/DESIGN FIRM

MATT KLIM/ART DIRECTOR

MATT KLIM, PETER KLIMKIEWICZ/DESIGNERS

PETER FIORE/ILLUSTRATOR

2.

2. MASSENEZ LIQUEURS

G.E. MASSENEZ (FRANCE)/CLIENT

SUSAN MESHBERG GRAPHIC DESIGN/DESIGN FIRM

SUSAN MESHBERG/ART DIRECTOR-DESIGNER

PAUL CALABRO/ILLUSTRATOR

3.

4.

5.

3. MICHELOB GOLDEN
4. O'DOUL'S
ANHEUSER-BUSCH INC/CLIENT
OBATA DESIGN/DESIGN FIRM

5. CLUSS
BRAUEREI CLUSS/CLIENT
KNUT HARTMANN DESIGN/DESIGN FIRM
KNUT HARTMANN/ART DIRECTOR-DESIGNER
HEINZ SCHULTCHEN/ILLUSTRATOR

6.

6. SCORPION DRY LAGER

VAUX BREWERIES/CLIENT

ELMWOOD/DESIGN FIRM

GARY SWINDELL/ART DIRECTOR-DESIGNER

7.

7. LISMORE WHISKY

WILLIAM LUNDIE & CO LTD/CLIENT

GRAPHIC PARTNERS/DESIGN FIRM

GRAHAM DUFFY/ART DIRECTOR-DESIGNER

8. BOHEMIA BEER

CERVECERIA CUAUHTEMOC S.A./CLIENT

ADVANCE DESIGN CENTER/DESIGN FIRM

JAIME SENDRA/ART DIRECTOR-DESIGNER

8.

10.

9.

9. MONTEGO BAY RUM LABELS

BARUH SPIRITS/CLIENT

BRAD BARUH/ART DIRECTOR

DENIS KLIENE/DESIGNER

RALPH BAKER/ILLUSTRATOR

10. JACQUES BONET

CHRISTIAN BROTHERS/CLIENT

BROOM & BROOM INC/DESIGN FIRM

DAVID BROOM/ART DIRECTOR-DESIGNER

12.

12. SERRANO & DORADO TACCONI

13. BIANCOSARTI LIGHT APERITIF

14. BIANCOSARTI APERITIF

ERVEN LUCAS BOLS S.A./CLIENT

ESTUDIO HACHE S.A./DESIGN FIRM

LAURA LAZZERETTI, MARCELO VARELA/DESIGNERS

13.

14.

15.

15. ISLE OF JURA WHISKY

INVERGORDON DISTILLERS GROUP/CLIENT

GRAPHIC PARTNERS/DESIGN FIRM

RON BURNETT/ART DIRECTOR-DESIGNER

ROSAMUND FOWLER/ILLUSTRATOR

16. ASBACH SELECTION

ASBACH & CO WEINBRENNEREI/CLIENT

KNUT HARTMANN DESIGN/DESIGN FIRM

KNUT HARTMANN/ART DIRECTOR

THOMAS SKUJAT/DESIGNER-ILLUSTRATOR

WERNER WALTER/PHOTOGRAPHER

17. POINT ROYALE

HEUBLEIN INC/CLIENT

KLIM DESIGN/DESIGN FIRM

MATT KLIM/ART DIRECTOR

PETER KLIMKIEWICZ, DON MARTIN/DESIGNERS

18. HAPPY VALLEY BREW

HAPPY VALLEY BREWERY/CLIENT

SOMMESE DESIGN/DESIGN FIRM

LANNY SOMMESE/ART DIRECTOR-ILLUSTRATOR

KRISTEN SOMMESE/DESIGNER

16.

17.

18.

19. THE ORIGINAL MACKINLAY WHISKY
INVERGORDON DISTILLERS GROUP/CLIENT
GRAPHIC PARTNERS/DESIGN FIRM
RON BURNETT/ART DIRECTOR-DESIGNER

20. THE INVERGORDON
INVERGORDON DISTILLERS GROUP/CLIENT
GRAPHIC PARTNERS/DESIGN FIRM
RON BURNETT/ART DIRECTOR-DESIGNER
JEREMY SANCHA/ILLUSTRATOR

19.

20.

21.

BEER / LIQUOR

21. CUERVO GIFT CARTON

HEUBLEIN INC/CLIENT

MITTLEMAN-ROBINSON INC/DESIGN FIRM

FRED MITTLEMAN/ART DIRECTOR

RICHARD BRANDT/DESIGNER

22.

22. CINZANO VERMOUTH

PADDINGTON/CLIENT

MITTLEMAN-ROBINSON INC/DESIGN FIRM

FRED MITTLEMAN/ART DIRECTOR-DESIGNER

Wine

I LEARNED AN IMPORTANT LESSON IN LABEL DESIGN TWELVE YEARS AGO. *DON'T OVERSOPHISTICATE A*

LABEL DESIGN AND BOOST IT INTO A HIGHER CATEGORY IF THE PRODUCT DOESN'T WARRANT IT. UNDER

CLIENT DIRECTIVES, WE DID *EXACTLY* THAT FOR A WINERY AND, WITHIN MONTHS OF THE NEW LABEL

INTRODUCTION, SALES DROPPED. IT WAS DETERMINED THAT THE CONSUMER WHO WAS LOOKING FOR

AN INEXPENSIVE WINE OVERLOOKED THIS NEW LABEL BECAUSE IT LOOKED TOO EXPENSIVE. THE MORE

EXPERIENCED WINE BUYER, LOOKING FOR A BETTER WINE, PURCHASED IT AND FOUND IT DID NOT LIVE

UP TO ITS IMAGE. THAT ACCOUNTED FOR THE LOSS OF A REPEAT PURCHASE. ALTHOUGH TRADITIONAL

DESIGN IS APPROPRIATE FOR TRADITIONAL VARIETALS, TRENDIER, MORE COLORFUL DESIGN WORKS,

BETTER WHEN INTRODUCING FRESHER WINES LIKE THE NOUVEAUS AND LIGHTER VARIETALS. FOR A

LABEL DESIGN TO BE SUCCESSFUL, IT SHOULD NOT ONLY BE THE BEST IT CAN BE, BUT... MORE IMPOR-

TANTLY, IT MUST BE APPROPRIATE FOR THE PRODUCT.

Rick Tharp, Designer/Art Director,
THARP DID IT

1.

1. APEX WINE
ALHADEFF DISTRIBUTING CO/CLIENT
TIM GIRVIN DESIGN INC/DESIGN FIRM
TIM GIRVIN/ART DIRECTOR
TIM GIRVIN, ANTON KIMBALL/DESIGNERS

2.

2. MWDL SELF-PROMOTIONAL WINE
MURRIE, WHITE, DRUMMOND, LIENHART/
DESIGN FIRM
LINDA VOLL/ART DIRECTOR-DESIGNER-
ILLUSTRATOR
PAUL RUNG/PHOTOGRAPHER

3. GUSTAVE NIEBAUM

INGLENOOK/CLIENT

COLONNA FARRELL DESIGN/DESIGN FIRM

JOHN FARRELL/ART DIRECTOR-ILLUSTRATOR

AMY RACINA/DESIGNER

DAVID BISHOP/PHOTOGRAPHER

4.

3.

4. LYETH

VINTECH WINE GROUP/CLIENT

COLONNA FARRELL DESIGN/DESIGN FIRM

RALPH COLONNA/ART DIRECTOR-DESIGNER

DAVID BISHOP/PHOTOGRAPHER

5.

6.

7.

5. HANNS KORNELL BLANC DE NOIRS

HANNS KORNELL/CLIENT

COLONNA FARRELL DESIGN/DESIGN FIRM

TONY AUSTON, RICHARD CLARK/ART DIRECTORS

AMY RACINA/DESIGNER

DAVID BISHOP/PHOTOGRAPHER

6. LAURIER CHARDONNAY

VINTECH WINE GROUP/CLIENT

COLONNA FARRELL DESIGN/DESIGN FIRM

CYNTHIA MAGUIRE, RALPH COLONNA/ART
 DIRECTORS

AMY RACINA/DESIGNER

DAVID BISHOP/PHOTOGRAPHER

7. SALMON CREEK CHARDONNAY

SALMON CREEK/CLIENT

COLONNA FARRELL DESIGN/DESIGN FIRM

RALPH COLONNA/ART DIRECTOR

SUSAN HANDLEY/DESIGNER

DAVID BISHOP/PHOTOGRAPHER

8. LAS VINAS

LAS VINAS/CLIENT

COLONNA FARRELL DESIGN/DESIGN FIRM

TONY AUSTON/ART DIRECTOR, DESIGNER

ROSE HODGES/PHOTOGRAPHER

8

9.

10.

11.

9. COTES DU SONOMA CABERNET

PELLEGRINI VINEYARDS/CLIENT

COLONNA FARRELL DESIGN/DESIGN FIRM

RALPH COLONNA/ART DIRECTOR

CYNTHIA MAGUIRE/DESIGNER

MICHELLE MANNING/ILLUSTRATOR

DAVID BISHOP/PHOTOGRAPHER

10. CHARLES SHAW PINOT NOIR

CHARLES SHAW/CLIENT

COLONNA FARRELL DESIGN/DESIGN FIRM

RALPH COLONNA/ART DIRECTOR

AMY RACINA/DESIGNER

BETH LEEDS/ILLUSTRATOR

DAVID BISHOP/PHOTOGRAPHER

11. BYRON PINOT NOIR

BYRON VINEYARDS/CLIENT

COLONNA FARRELL DESIGN/DESIGN FIRM

RALPH COLONNA/ART DIRECTOR

TONY AUSTON, PEGGY KOCH/DESIGNERS

DAVID BISHOP/PHOTOGRAPHER

15.

15. NAPA RIDGE

BERINGER VINEYARDS/CLIENT

BROOM & BROOM INC/DESIGN FIRM

DAVID BROOM/ART DIRECTOR-DESIGNER

12.

13.

14.

12. ST. GREGORY CHARDONNAY
ST. GREGORY/CLIENT
COLONNA FARRELL DESIGN/DESIGN FIRM
TONY AUSTON/ART DIRECTOR
AMY RACINA/DESIGNER
DAVID BISHOP/PHOTOGRAPHER

13. MAISON DEUTZ CHAMPAGNE
WINE WORLD/CLIENT
COLONNA FARRELL DESIGN/DESIGN FIRM
RALPH COLONNA/ART DIRECTOR
SUSAN HANDLEY/DESIGNER
DAVID BISHOP/PHOTOGRAPHER

14. DE LOS CAMPOS RED TABLE WINE
CHARLES SHAW/CLIENT
COLONNA FARRELL DESIGN/DESIGN FIRM
RALPH COLONNA, CYNTHIA MAGUIRE/ART
 DIRECTORS
AMY RACINA/DESIGNER
BETH LEEDS/ILLUSTRATOR

16.

16. KNAPP VINEYARDS CHAMPAGNE
KNAPP VINEYARDS/CLIENT
LOUISE FILI LTD/DESIGN FIRM
LOUISE FILI/ART DIRECTOR-DESIGNER
PHILIPPE WEISBECKER/ILLUSTRATOR

17.

17. MARSHALL FIELD'S GOURMET WINES

MARSHALL FIELD'S/CLIENT

MURRIE, WHITE, DRUMMOND, LIENHART/

 DESIGN FIRM

WAYNE KRIMSTON/ART DIRECTOR-DESIGNER

DON TATE/ILLUSTRATOR

HORST MICKLER/HAND LETTERING

PAUL RUNG/PHOTOGRAPHER

18

18. MONTANA STREET CAFE WINE

JOHN DAVIS/CLIENT

MURRIE, WHITE, DRUMMOND, LIENHART/

 DESIGN FIRM

LINDA VOLL/ART DIRECTOR-DESIGNER-ILLUSTRATOR

PAUL RUNG/PHOTOGRAPHER

19.

19. TRAPICHE WINES
VINOS ARGENTINOS/CLIENT
MITTLEMAN-ROBINSON INC/DESIGN FIRM
FRED MITTLEMAN/ART DIRECTOR-DESIGNER

20.

20. PIEDMONT GROCERY LABELS
THE PIEDMONT GROCERY/CLIENT
EMERY-POE DESIGN/DESIGN FIRM
DAVID POE/ART DIRECTOR
DAVID POE, JONATHAN MULCARE/DESIGNERS-
  ILLUSTRATORS

21. WINDSOR PRIVATE RESERVE WINE LABEL
AND GIFT BOX
WINDSOR VINEYARDS/CLIENT
JON WELLS ASSOC/DESIGN FIRM
JON WELLS/DESIGNER

21.

22.

22. THOMAS YEAGER

THOMAS YEAGER WINERY/CLIENT

THE WELLER INSTITUTE FOR THE CURE OF DESIGN/
 DESIGN FIRM

DON YOUNG/ART DIRECTOR

DON WELLER, DON YOUNG/DESIGNERS

DON WELLER/ILLUSTRATOR

23.

24.

24. HEICHINROU RESTAURANT HOUSE WINE

HEICHINROU RESTAURANT/CLIENT

ALAN CHAN DESIGN CO/DESIGN FIRM

ALAN CHAN/ART DIRECTOR

ALAN CHAN, ALVIN CHAN/DESIGNERS

23. CLOS ST. THOMAS
CLOS ST. THOMAS VINEYARDS/CLIENT
AKAGI DESIGN/DESIGN FIRM
DOUG AKAGI/ART DIRECTOR
KIMBERLY POWELL/DESIGNER

25. ABREU WINE
ABREU VINEYARDS/CLIENT
ORTEGA DESIGN/DESIGN FIRM
JOANN & SUSANN ORTEGA/ART DIRECTORS-
 DESIGNERS
ROBERT SWARTLEY/ILLUSTRATOR-ENGRAVER

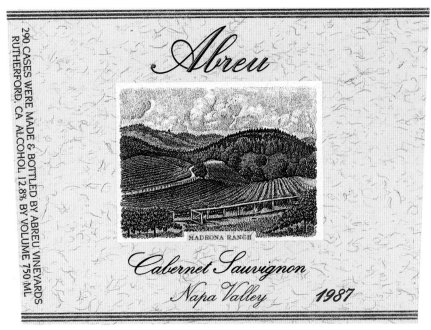

25 .

26. SURDYK'S WINE
SURDYK'S/CLIENT
WILLIAM HOMAN DESIGN/DESIGN FIRM
WILLIAM HOMAN/ART DIRECTOR-DESIGNER

26.

27. JORDAN "J" CHAMPAGNE

JORDAN SPARKLING WINE CO/CLIENT

COLONNA FARRELL DESIGN/DESIGN FIRM

RALPH COLONNA, TOM JORDAN/ART DIRECTORS

RALPH COLONNA, PEGGY KOCH/DESIGNERS

MICHAEL LAMOTTEE/PHOTOGRAPHER

27.

WINE

28. PAT PAULSEN WINE

PAT PAULSEN WINERY/CLIENT

COGNATA ASSOC/DESIGN FIRM

RICHARD COGNATA/ART DIRECTOR-DESIGNER

28.

29. NOBILO CONCEPT 2

HOUSE OF NOBILO/CLIENT

COLONNA FARRELL DESIGN/DESIGN FIRM

RALPH COLONNA/ART DIRECTOR

PEGGY KOCH/DESIGNER

MIKE GRAY/ILUSTRATOR

DAVID BISHOP/PHOTOGRAPHER

29.

Beverages

FOR THOSE CONCERNED ABOUT THE ISSUES OF DESIGN AND ETHICS, THE SINGLE MOST CHALLENGING

ASPECT OF PACKAGING IS THE QUESTION OF BEING RESPONSIBLE TO THE CONSUMER. PACKAGES

DESIGNED TO DELIBERATELY MISREPRESENT THEIR CONTENTS AND CREATE EXPECTATIONS THAT CAN-

NOT BE REALIZED CREATE AN ETHICAL DILEMMA FOR THE DESIGNER. IF WE CONSIDER THE AUDIENCE

TO CONSIST OF OUR FRIENDS, NEIGHBORS, AND RELATIVES RATHER THAN AN UNIDENTIFIED "MARKET OF

ANONYMOUS BUYERS," OUR ATTITUDE TOWARD THE ACTIVITY CHANGES. IT MOVES FROM BECOMING A

PROFESSIONAL TASK TO A SOCIAL ONE. WE SEEM TO BE AT A MOMENT IN HISTORY WHERE THIS SHIFT

IN ATTITUDE AND THE DEFINITION OF WHAT SERVES THE COMMON GOOD IS CRITICAL. ❧ IT IS NO

LONGER APPROPRIATE FOR THOSE OF US INVOLVED IN PACKAGING AND OTHER FORMS OF PUBLIC COM-

MUNICATION TO BE UNAWARE OF THE CONSEQUENCES OF OUR WORK. WELCOME TO THE MILLENNIUM.

Milton Glaser, President
Milton Glaser Inc

1.

1. 24 CARAT FREEZE DRIED COFFEE
ELITE INDUSTRIES LTD/CLIENT
VARDIMON DESIGN/DESIGN FIRM
YAROM VARDIMON/ART DIRECTOR-DESIGNER

2.

2. CAPPIO ICED COFFEE
KRAFT, GENERAL FOODS/CLIENT
MITTLEMAN-ROBINSON INC/DESIGN FIRM
FRED MITTLEMAN/ART DIRECTOR
RICHARD BRANDT/DESIGNER

3.

3. SIMON DAVID COFFEE

COLONIAL COFFEE/CLIENT

ADVANCE DESIGN CENTER/DESIGN FIRM

JAIME SENDRA/ART DIRECTOR

BRYAN ROGERS/DESIGNER

4.

4. BEACH CLUB CLEAR JUICE SPARKLER

NEW ERA BEVERAGE CO/CLIENT

ADVANCE DESIGN CENTER/DESIGN FIRM

JAIME SENDRA/ART DIRECTOR

BRYAN ROGERS/DESIGNER

BILL HALL/ILLUSTRATOR

5.

5. MELROSE'S ORGANICALLY GROWN COFFEE

PREMIER BRANDS/CLIENT

GRAPHIC PARTNERS/DESIGN FIRM

KEN CRAIG/ART DIRECTOR-DESIGNER

DOVRAT BEN-NAHUM/ILLUSTRATOR

6.

6. TEA PACKAGING-MANDARIN ORIENTAL HOTEL

7. COFFEE TIN-MANDARIN ORIENTAL HOTEL

MANDARIN ORIENTAL H.K./CLIENT

ALAN CHAN DESIGN CO/DESIGN FIRM

ALAN CHAN/ART DIRECTOR

ALAN CHAN, PHILLIP LEUNG/DESIGNERS

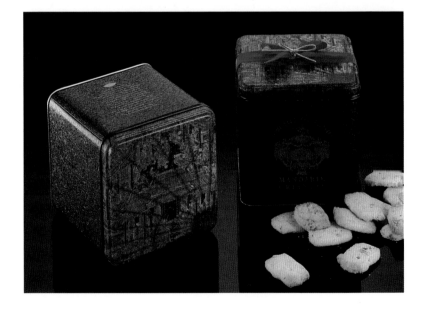

7.

8. EVERFRESH FRUIT BEVERAGES
JOHN LABATT LTD/CLIENT
LIPSON-ALPORT-GLASS & ASSOC/DESIGN FIRM

8.

9. SANTA MARIA BOTTLED WATER
MANANTIALES S.A. DE C.V./CLIENT
ADVANCE DESIGN CENTER/DESIGN FIRM
JAIME SENDRA/ART DIRECTOR
BRYAN ROGERS/DESIGNER

9.

10.

10. EVERFRESH SPARKLING MINERAL WATER

WITH FRUIT JUICE

JOHN LABATT LTD/CLIENT

LIPSON-ALPORT-GLASS & ASSOC/DESIGN FIRM

11.

11. MACAW TRADITIONAL LEMONDADE

MACAW LTD/CLIENT

ELMWOOD/DESIGN FIRM

JULIA WHITE/ART DIRECTOR-DESIGNER

JOHN RICHARDSON/ILLUSTRATOR

12. TETLEY ROUND TEA BAGS

TETLEY INC/CLIENT

PETERSON & BLYTH ASSOC/DESIGN FIRM

RONALD PETERSON/ART DIRECTOR

JOE VIOLANTE/DESIGNERS

12.

13. LIPTON TEAS

THOMAS J. LIPTON INC/CLIENT

MURRIE, WHITE, DRUMMOND, LIENHART/
DESIGN FIRM

JAYCE DOUGALL SCHMIDT/ART DIRECTOR-DESIGNER

PAUL RUNG/PHOTOGRAPHER

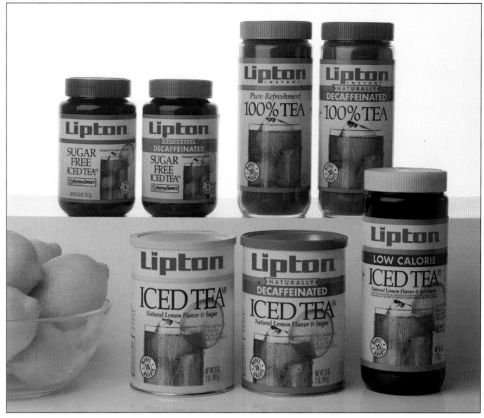

13.

14. CHIQUITA 100% JUICE BLENDS

CHIQUITA BRANDS INTERNATIONAL/CLIENT

LIPSON-ALPORT-GLASS & ASSOC/DESIGN FIRM

14.

15.

15. DEER PARK

THE CLOROX COMPANY/CLIENT

COLEMAN, LIPUMA, SEGAL & MORRILL INC/

 DESIGN FIRM

OWEN W. COLEMAN, ABE SEGAL/CREATIVE

 DIRECTORS

OWEN W. COLEMAN, JOHN RUTIG, ABE SEGAL/

 DESIGNERS

16.

16. CRYSTAL, ALHAMBRA AND SPARKLETTS

MCKESSON WATER PRODUCTS COMPANY/CLIENT

COLEMAN, LIPUMA, SEGAL & MORRILL INC/

 DESIGN FIRM

OWEN W. COLEMAN, ABE SEGAL/CREATIVE

 DIRECTORS

OWEN W. COLEMAN, WILLIAM LEE, JOHN RUTIG/

 DESIGNERS

17.

Snacks

PACKAGING DESIGN IS THE PRE-EMINENT MARKETING TOOL—IT MAKES MONEY. PACKAGING IS THE ONLY

EVIDENCE OF THE TOTAL MARKETING EFFORT. PACKAGING HAS A LIFE LONGER THAN ANY MARKETING

CAMPAIGN. PACKAGING EXISTS WITHOUT ADVERTISING, THE OPPOSITE IS IMPOSSIBLE. PACKAGING IS

THE ONLY SALES MOTIVATOR SEEN BY THE CONSUMERS, BEFORE, DURING, AND AFTER PURCHASE THAN

ANY OTHER MARKETING EFFORT. PACKAGING'S PRIMARY PURPOSE IS TO COMPEL CONSUMERS TO BUY.

PACKAGING IS THE LAST AND ONLY CONNECTION BETWEEN COMPANY AND CONSUMER AT THE POINT OF

SALE. PACKAGING REMAINS WITH THE CONSUMER DURING THE PRODUCT LIFE. DURING THAT TIME PACK-

AGING MENTALLY REINFORCES BRAND AWARENESS, PRODUCT EFFICACY AND RE-PURCHASE MOTIVATION.

PACKAGING DESIGN *IS* THE AD, E.G., DOWBRANDS' SCRUBBING BUBBLES. PACKAGING IS SO UBIQUITOUS

IT'S INVISIBLE. BY NOT RECOGNIZING THAT TRUISM—A MARKETER MISSES THE SOLUTION TO A MYRIAD

OF PROBLEMS AND GREATER PROFIT.

Alan W. Anderson, Managing Partner,
Package Design of America

1.

SNACKS

1. ALMOND PLAZA

BLUE DIAMOND/CLIENT

PAGE DESIGN INC/DESIGN FIRM

PAUL PAGE/ART DIRECTOR

PAULA SUGARMAN/DESIGNER-ILLUSTRATOR

KENT LAGIN/PHOTOGRAPHER

2. POPCORN CANISTERS

CALIFORNIA ALMOND GROWERS/CLIENT

PAGE DESIGN INC/DESIGN FIRM

PAUL PAGE/ART DIRECTOR

TRACY TITUS/DESIGNER

2.

3.

3. CLASSIC CHOCOLATE

ELITE INDUSTRIES LTD/CLIENT

VARDIMON DESIGN/DESIGN FIRM

YAROM VARDIMON/ART DIRECTOR-DESIGNER

EDDA GUDNASON/ILLUSTRATOR

3.

3. SAFEWAY SNACKS
SAFEWAY/CLIENT
TRICKETT & WEBB/DESIGN FIRM-ILLUSTRATORS
BRIAN WEBB, LYNN TRICKETT, ANDREW THOMAS/
 DESIGNERS

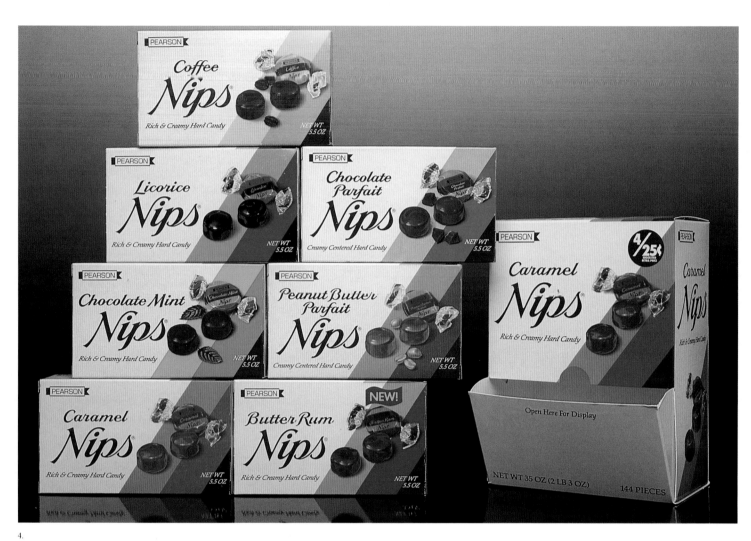

4.

4. NIPS CANDIES

NESTLE FOODS CORP/CLIENT

MITTLEMAN-ROBINSON INC/DESIGN FIRM

FRED MITTLEMAN/ART DIRECTOR-DESIGNER

JULIA NOONAN/ILLUSTRATOR

5.

5. CRYSTAL LIGHT BARS

GENERAL FOODS/CLIENT

JOEL BRONZ DESIGN/DESIGN FIRM

JOEL BRONZ/ART DIRECTOR

KAREN WILLOUGHBY/DESIGNER

6.

6. BISCOTTI LABELS

BISCOTTI COOKIE CO/CLIENT

PUCCINELLI DESIGN/DESIGN FIRM

KEITH PUCCINELLI/ART DIRECTOR-DESIGNER-

 ILLUSTRATOR

7.

8.

7. MILLER'S THINS & CARR'S TABLE WATER BISCUITS

UNITED BISCUITS/CLIENT

ELMWOOD/DESIGN FIRM

JULIA WHITE/ART DIRECTOR-DESIGNER

SUE HISCOE/PHOTOGRAPHER

8. CHILI CON QUESO DIP

THE BACHMAN COMPANY/CLIENT

DIXON & PARCELS ASSOC INC/DESIGN FIRM

9. NESTLE CHOCOLATE BARS

NESTLE FOODS CORP/CLIENT

MURRIE, WHITE, DRUMMOND, LIENHART/
 DESIGN FIRM

THOMAS Q. WHITE/ART DIRECTOR-DESIGNER

9.

10. FRANGO CHOCOLATES

MARSHALL FIELD'S/CLIENT

MURRIE WHITE DRUMMOND LIENHART/DESIGN FIRM

WAYNE KRIMSTON/ART DIRECTOR-DESIGNER

DON TATE/ILLUSTRATOR

HORST MICKLER/HAND LETTERING

PAUL RUNG/PHOTOGRAPHER

10.

SNACKS

11. MARSHALL FIELD'S GOURMET NUTS
MARSHALL FIELD'S/CLIENT
MURRIE, WHITE, DRUMMOND, LIENHART/
 DESIGN FIRM
WAYNE KRIMSTON/ART DIRECTOR-DESIGNER
DON TATE/ILLUSTRATOR
HORST MICKLER/HAND LETTERING

11.

12. KRAFT TOPPINGS
KRAFT INC/CLIENT
MURRIE, WHITE, DRUMMOND, LIENHART/
 DESIGN FIRM
JEFF WHITE/ART DIRECTOR-DESIGNER
PAUL RUNG/PHOTOGRAPHER

12.

13.

13. MINUTE MAID FRUIT JUICEE FROZEN SNACKS
COCA-COLA FOODS/CLIENT
MURRIE, WHITE, DRUMMOND, LIENHART/
 DESIGN FIRM
WAYNE KRIMSTON, JAYCE DOUGALL SCHMIDT/
 ART DIRECTORS-DESIGNERS

14. MARSHALL FIELD'S GOURMET NUTS
MARSHALL FIELD'S/CLIENT
MURRIE, WHITE, DRUMMOND, LIENHART/
 DESIGN FIRM
WAYNE KRIMSTON, CHERYL EJI/ART DIRECTORS-
 DESIGNERS
DON TATE/ILLUSTRATOR
HORST MICKLER/HAND LETTERING
PAUL RUNG/PHOTOGRAPHER

14.

15.

15. COLOMBO SHOPPE STYLE SOFT FROZEN YOGURT

COLOMBO INCORPORATED/CLIENT

HILLIS MACKEY & CO/DESIGN FIRM

TERRY MACKEY/ART DIRECTOR-DESIGNER-

 ILLUSTRATOR

TODD AP JONES/HAND LETTERING

MATRE RAJTAR, TOM MATRE/PHOTOGRAPHER

16. BAHLSEN MILK & DARK CHOCOLATE

LIEBNIZ COOKIES

BAHLSEN INC/CLIENT

DIXON & PARCELS ASSOCIATES INC/DESIGN FIRM

16.

17.

17. CAMILLE BLOCH CHOCOLATES
CHOCOLATS CAMILLE BLOCH S.A./CLIENT
GERSTMAN+MEYERS INC/DESIGN FIRM
HERBERT M. MEYERS/OVERALL SUPERVISOR
JUAN CONCEPCION/CREATIVE DIRECTOR
LARRY RIDDELL/DESIGN DIRECTOR

17A.

17A. TEDDY GRAHAMS GRAHAM SNACKS
NABISCO/CLIENT
GERSTMAN+MEYERS INC/DESIGN FIRM
RICHARD GERSTMAN/OVERALL SUPERVISOR
JUAN CONCEPCION/CREATIVE SUPERVISOR
RAFAEL FELICIANO/DESIGN DIRECTOR
JERRY DIOR, RIC HIRST/DESIGNERS

18.

18. SAROTTI

NESTLE CHOCOLADEN GmbH/CLIENT

KNUT HARTMANN DESIGN/DESIGN FIRM

ROLAND MEHLER/ART DIRECTOR-DESIGNER-ILLUSTRATOR

HANS BELL, SUSANNE OBERAUER/DESIGNERS

GOTTHART EICHHORN/PHOTOGRAPHER

19.

19. CREME DE LA CREME

LUZIANNE BLUE PLATE FOODS/CLIENT

GERTMAN+MEYERS INC/DESIGN FIRM

RICHARD GERSTMAN/OVERALL SUPERVISOR

JUAN CONCEPCION/CREATIVE DIRECTOR

RAFAEL FELICIANO/DESIGN DIRECTOR

KIM KOLLBERG/DESIGNER

20.

20. PETITS COEURS COOKIES

CHOCOOKY PREMIUM COOKIES

FLEISCHMANN E ROYAL, NABISCO/CLIENT

DIL CONSULTANTS IN DESIGN/DESIGN FIRM

DIL DESIGN TEAM/ART DIRECTORS

21.

21. SADIA HAM AND LIVER PATE

SADIA COMERCIAL S.A./CLIENT

DIL CONSULTANTS IN DESIGN/DESIGN FIRM

DIL DESIGN TEAM/ART DIRECTORS

22.

22. MONIQUE'S CAKE SHOP

QUALITY BAKER PTE LTD/CLIENT

ALAN CHAN DESIGN CO/DESIGN FIRM

ALAN CHAN/ART DIRECTOR

ALAN CHAN, CETRIC LEUNG/DESIGNERS

DEE DEE CHOY/ILLUSTRATOR

23.

23. FISHER NUTS

PROCTOR & GAMBLE CO/CLIENT

LIPSON-ALPORT-GLASS & ASSOC/DESIGN FIRM

24.

24. HEATH ENGLISH TOFFEE BARS

LEAF INC/CLIENT

LIPSON-ALPORT-GLASS & ASSOC/DESIGN FIRM

25. NESTLE ALPINE WHITE

NESTLE FOODS CORP/CLIENT

HANS FLINK DESIGN INC/DESIGN FIRM

HANS D. FLINK, RON VANDENBERG/ART DIRECTORS

AMY ATKINSON/DESIGNER

26. METROPOLIS FINE CONFECTIONS

BAGGED CANDIES

SAMBEVE SPECIALTY FOODS/CLIENT

THE DESIGN COMPANY/DESIGN FIRM

MARCIA ROMANUCK/ART DIRECTOR-DESIGNER-

  PHOTOGRAPHER

27. METROPOLIS FINE CONFECTIONS

ASSORTED TRUFFLES

SAMBEVE SPECIALTY FOODS/CLIENT

THE DESIGN COMPANY/DESIGN FIRM

MARCIA ROMANUCK/ART DIRECTOR-DESIGNER

BARRY ARONSON/PHOTOGRAPHER

25.

26.

27.

28.

28. GEORGE BAXTER'S CELLAR & MRS. BAXTER'S

VICTORIAN KITCHEN CONFECTIONARY

BAXTER'S/CLIENT

GRAPHIC PARTNERS/DESIGN FIRM

KEN CRAIG/ART DIRETOR

KATE STOCKWELL/DESIGNER

29.

29. MRS. MCALLISTER'S BISCUITS

SIMMERS/CLIENT

GRAPHIC PARTNERS/DESIGN FIRM

KEN CRAIG/ART DIRECTOR

KATE STOCKWELL/DESIGNER

CLAIRE HEWITT/ILLUSTRATOR

30.

SNACKS

30. FRITOS CORN CHIPS

FRITO-LAY INC/CLIENT

APPLE DESIGNSOURCE INC/DESIGN FIRM

BARRY G. SEELIG/ART DIRECTOR

NANCY BROGDEN, CHAVA BEN-AMOS, KAREN

 WILLOUGHBY/DESIGNERS

31.

31. REDDI-WHIP

BEATRICE/CLIENT

MICHAEL STANARD INC/DESIGN FIRM

MICHAEL STANARD/ART DIRECTOR-DESIGNER

Foods

NOVEMBER 15, 1991. I WAS ON MY WAY TO TOKYO AFTER A CONFERENCE SESSION IN KOBE. HUNGER

CAUGHT ON AND I BOUGHT A 'BENTO', THE JAPANESE LUNCH BOX, BEFORE BOARDING THE TRAIN. I

SOON DISCOVERED THE HEXAGONAL-SHAPED CARDBOARD PACK WHICH HOUSED A HOST OF MYSTERIOUS

PLEASURES. FIRST, I HAD TO PULL THE PLASTIC "TONGUE" WHICH WOULD START THE CHEMICAL PROCESS

OF HEATING UP THE CONTENTS INSIDE THE POLYMERIZED BOX IN 8 MINUTES. WHILE HOLDING THE BOX AS

IT GOT HOTTER, I COULD NOT HELP FEELING A CHILDLIKE EXCITEMENT FOR WHAT WAS TO COME: I WOULD

HAVE RICE WITH *FRUITS DE MER* AND EAT LIKE A KING—AT LEAST LIKE THE KING OF HARIMA OF THE

REGION, AS THE PACKAGE SAID. AFTER THE MEAL, I COULD HAVE THE CLAY FIGURINE WHISTLE THAT

CAME WITH THE LUNCH BOX TO TAKE HOME AS A SOUVENIR. AND IT GAVE ME FOOD FOR THOUGHT AS

WELL. IT IS FUNCTIONALLY DESIGNED AS A CONTAINER; IT HAS ELEMENTS OF NOVELTY AND APPEAL; IT

TYPIFIES THE OLD MEETING THE NEW; AND IT CATERS TO THE MODERN NEW PHILOSOPHY FOR PACKAGE

DESIGN! I FELT A COMMUNION WITH THIS ANONYMOUS COLLEAGUE OF THE TRADE.

Alan Chan, Creative Director,
Alan Chan Design Company

TESCO CAN NOW OFFER YOU NATURALLY GROWN PRODUCE FROM AROUND THE WORLD.

OUR ORGANIC FRUITS AND VEGETABLES ARE GROWN TO STANDARDS MONITORED BY TESCO AND THE ORGANIC GROWERS SOIL ASSOCIATION IN FIELDS AND ORCHARDS FREE FROM ARTIFICIAL CHEMICAL PESTI-CIDES AND FERTILIZERS FOR AT LEAST TWO YEARS.

THE TESCO RANGE IS GROWN USING NATURAL COMPOST FERTILIZERS AND IS IDEAL FOR THOSE CONCERNED ABOUT CHEMICAL RESIDUES AND THE ENVIRONMENT.

THE PRODUCE HAS A NATURAL APPEARANCE AND IS A LITTLE MORE EXPENSIVE THAN OUR CONVENTIONAL RANGE. THIS IS BECAUSE IT IS MORE DIFFICULT TO GROW CROPS USING ONLY NATURAL METHODS.

TRY OUR NEW RANGE BY LOOKING OUT FOR THIS LOGO

1.

1 TESCO FRESH FRUITS & VEGETABLES

TESCO/CLIENT

TRICKETT & WEBB/DESIGN FIRM

BRIAN WEBB, LYNN TRICKETT, AVRIL BROADLEY,

 SARAH MATTINSON/DESIGNERS

GLYNN BOYD HART, PAUL LEITH/ILLUSTRATORS

2.

2. MANDARIN ORIENTAL FOODS

MANDARIN ORIENTAL H.K./CLIENT

ALAN CHAN DESIGN CO/DESIGN FIRM

ALAN CHAN/ART DIRECTOR

ALAN CHAN, PHILLIP LEUNG/DESIGNER

3.

3. TREASURE CAVE BRIE

BEATRICE/CLIENT

MICHAEL STANARD INC/DESIGN FIRM

MICHAEL STANARD/ART DIRECTOR

ANN WERNER/DESIGNER

4.

4. YOUNG'S PRAWN COCKTAIL
YOUNG'S CHILLED FISH/CLIENT
ELMWOOD/DESIGN FIRM
CLARE MARSH/ART DIRECTOR-DESIGNER-
 ILLUSTRATOR
HEATHER BROWN/PHOTOGRAPHER

5. ITALIA

ITALIA RESTAURANTS/CLIENT

HORNALL ANDERSON DESIGN WORKS/DESIGN FIRM

JACK ANDERSON/ART DIRECTOR

JACK ANDERSON, JULIA LAPINE/DESIGNERS

JULIA LAPINE/ILLUSTRATOR

6. PANE DI PAOLO ITALIAN BREAD

BROADMOOR BAKERY/CLIENT

HORNALL ANDERSON DESIGN WORKS/DESIGN FIRM

JACK ANDERSON/ART DIRECTOR

JACK ANDERSON, MARY HERMES/DESIGNERS

SCOTT MCDOUGAL/ILLUSTRATOR

5.

6.

7. VENECIA OIL AND VINEGAR

GOURMET AWARD FOODS/CLIENT

ADVANCE DESIGN CENTER/DESIGN FIRM

JAIME SENDRA/ART DIRECTOR

BRYAN ROGERS/DESIGNER

7.

8.

8. STANFORD COURT

STANFORD COURT/CLIENT

JAMIE DAVISON DESIGN INC/DESIGN FIRM

JAMIE DAVISON/ART DIRECTOR

JAMIE DAVISON, HEIDI STEVENS/DESIGNERS

9.

9. CHAUNCEY'S CHILI

CHAUNCEY'S CHILI/CLIENT

CLARK KELLER INC/DESIGN FIRM

JANE KELLER/ART DIRECTOR

NEAL M. ASHBY/DESIGNER-ILLUSTRATOR-
  HAND LETTERING

10. GURNEE MILLS APPLE BUTTER

WESTERN DEVELOPMENT CORP/CLIENT

COMMUNICATION ARTS INC/DESIGN FIRM

HENRY BEER/ART DIRECTOR

HUGH ENOCKSON/DESIGNER

10.

11. TIEDEMANN'S PEPPER JELLIES

TIEDEMANN'S/CLIENT

COLONNA FARRELL DESIGN/DESIGN FIRM

TONY AUSTON/ART DIRECTOR

PEGGY KOCH/DESIGNER

BETH LEEDS/ILLUSTRATOR

DAVID BISHOP/PHOTOGRAPHER

11.

12. BALDWIN HILL BREADS

BALDWIN HILL/CLIENT

THE DESIGN COMPANY/DESIGN FIRM

MARCIA ROMANUCK/ART DIRECTOR

MARCIA ROMANUCK, DENISE PICKERING/DESIGNERS

CHESAPEAKE STUDIOS/PHOTOGRAPHY

12.

13.

13. TERRITORIAL HOUSE SALSAS

PACE FOODS/CLIENT

GERSTMAN+MEYERS INC/DESIGN FIRM

RICHARD GERSTMAN/OVERALL SUPERVISOR

JUAN CONCEPCION/CREATIVE SUPERVISOR

LARRY RIDDELL/DESIGN DIRECTOR

JOANNA FELDHEIM/DESIGNER

14. LONE STAR GRILL SAUCES

MARSHALL FIELD'S/CLIENT

MURRIE, WHITE, DRUMMOND, LIENHART/
  DESIGN FIRM

AMY LEPPERT SHANNON/ART DIRECTOR-DESIGNER

TOM DUBOIS/ILLUSTRATOR

HORST MICKLER/HAND LETTERING

14.

15. LARRY MAHAN BBQ SAUCE & SALSA

CELEBRITY FOODS/CLIENT

PAGE DESIGN INC/DESIGN FIRM

PAUL PAGE/ART DIRECTOR

TRACY TITUS/DESIGNER-ILLUSTRATOR

16.

16. SUPRA

MOLINAS RIO DE LA PLATA/CLIENT

AVALOS & BOURSE/DESIGN FIRM

CARLOS AVALOS/ART DIRECTOR

ELVIO SANCHEZ/DESIGNER

15.

17.

17. PRATICE LINE BREADED CHICKEN PARTS

18. CALIFORNIA MEAT PRODUCTS

18A. MAXBURGER

SADIA COMERCIAL S.A./CLIENT

DIL CONSULTANTS IN DESIGN/DESIGN FIRM

DIL DESIGN TEAM/ART DIRECTORS

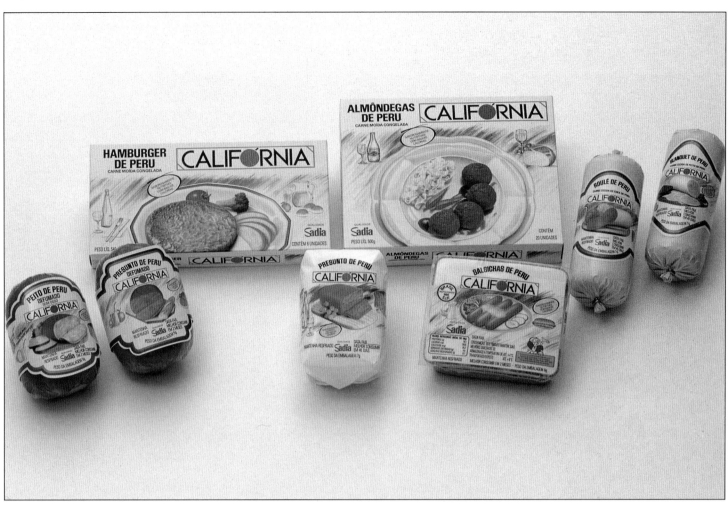

18.

18A.

19.

19. MARSHALL FIELD'S GOURMET JELLIES
& PRESERVES
MARSHALL FIELD'S/CLIENT
MURRIE, WHITE, DRUMMOND, LIENHART/DESIGN FIRM
WAYNE KRIMSTON/ART DIRECTOR-DESIGNER
DON TATE/ILLUSTRATOR

20. CHARLOTTE CHARLES
CHARLOTTE CHARLES INC/CLIENT
MURRIE, WHITE, DRUMMOND, LIENHART/
 DESIGN FIRM
LINDA VOLL/ART DIRECTOR-DESIGNER
GARY KELLEY/ILLUSTRATOR
PAUL RUNG/PHOTOGRAPHER

20.

21.

21. EUROPEAN ROYALTY PRESERVES
GOURMET AWARD FOODS/CLIENT
ADVANCE DESIGN CENTER/DESIGN FIRM
JAIME SENDRA/ART DIRECTOR
BRYAN ROGERS/DESIGNER
BILL HALL/ILLUSTRATOR

22.

22. LA PECHE DRESSINGS

LA PECHE/CLIENT

WALTER McCORD DESIGN/DESIGN FIRM

WALTER McCORD/ART DIRECTOR-DESIGNER-

 ILLUSTRATOR

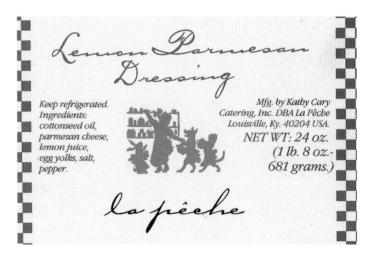

23. SONRITO'S BURRITOS

THE SOUTHLAND CORPORATION/CLIENT

ADVANCE DESIGN CENTER/DESIGN FIRM

JAIME SENDRA/ART DIRECTOR

DOUG LIVINGSTON/DESIGNER

24. RUDY'S FARM SAGE MILD & HOT SAUSAGES

RUDY'S FARM COMPANY/CLIENT

DIXON & PARCELS ASSOC INC/DESIGN FIRM

23.

24.

FOODS

25. CASA BUENA BURRITOS
THE SOUTHLAND CORPORATION/CLIENT
ADVANCE DESIGN CENTER/DESIGN FIRM
JAIME SENDRA/ART DIRECTOR
DOUG LIVINGSTON/DESIGNER

25.

26. EARTH GRAINS BREAD
CAMPBELL TAGGART INC/CLIENT
ADVANCE DESIGN CENTER/DESIGN FIRM
JAIME SENDRA/ART DIRECTOR
BRYAN ROGERS/DESIGNER

26.

27.

FOODS

28.

28. FRESHLIKE VEGETABLES

THE LARSEN CO/CLIENT

LIPSON-ALPORT-GLASS & ASSOC/DESIGN FIRM

ALLAN R. GLASS/ART DIRECTOR

LYLE ZIMMERMAN/DESIGNER

JOHN YOUSSI/ILLUSTRATOR

BILL BAKER/PHOTOGRAPHER

29. MARINADES IN MINUTES

RAGU FOODS INC/CLIENT

HANS FLINK DESIGN, INC/DESIGN FIRM

HANS D. FLINK/ART DIRECTOR

WILL MILLER/DESIGNER

DENNIS GOTTLIEB/PHOTOGRAPHER

29.

27. KNORR RISOTTOS

CPC INTERNATIONAL INC/CLIENT

GERSTMAN+MEYERS INC/DESIGN FIRM

RICHARD GERSTMAN/OVERALL SUPERVISOR

JUAN CONCEPCION/CREATIVE DIRECTOR

EILEEN STRAUSS/DESIGNER

30.

30. KINTARO FROZEN FOODS

KRAFT INC/CLIENT

MURRIE, WHITE, DRUMMOND, LIENHART/DESIGN FIRM

AMY LEPPERT SHANNON/ART DIRECTOR-DESIGNER

PAUL RUNG/PHOTOGRAPHER

31.

31. SARGENTO CHEESES

SARGENTO CHEESE CO/CLIENT

MURRIE, WHITE, DRUMMOND, LIENHART/DESIGN FIRM

THOMAS Q. WHITE/ART DIRECTOR-DESIGNER

PAUL RUNG/PHOTOGRAPHER

32.

32. FRESHAYR POTATO SACKS
FRESHAYR POTATOES/CLIENT
GRAPHIC PARTNERS/DESIGN FIRM
ANDREA WELSH/ART DIRECTOR-DESIGNER
IAIN MCINTOSH/ILLUSTRATOR

33.

33. EDEN SESAME SHAKE

EDEN FOODS INC/CLIENT

PERICH + PARTNERS/DESIGN FIRM

ERNIE PERICH/ART DIRECTOR

JANINE H. THIELK/DESIGNER

DAVE SCHWEITZER/ILLUSTRATOR

34.

34. LOUISA'S BASIL VINEGAR

CLASSICAL FOODS/CLIENT

LOUISE FILI LTD/DESIGN FIRM

LOUISE FILI/ART DIRECTOR-DESIGNER

SUSAN GABER/ILLUSTRATOR

35.

35. CUISINEL

CORMAN/CLIENT

B.E.P. DESIGN GROUP/DESIGN FIRM

BRIGITTE EVRARD/ART DIRECTOR

O. SALLY/DESIGNER

JEAN-PIERRE DE SIMPELAERE/ILLUSTRATOR

36.

36. MESSINIA OLIVE OIL

CLASSICAL FOODS/CLIENT

LOUISE FILI LTD/DESIGN FIRM

LOUISE FILI/ART DIRECTOR-DESIGNER

MELANIE PARKS/ILLUSTRATOR

37.

37. GLAZE

CONCORD FOODS INC/CLIENT

PACKAGE DESIGN OF AMERICA/DESIGN FIRM

ALAN ANDERSON, GARY HOLDA/DESIGNERS

CAPITAL PHOTO, STEVE MAAWED/PHOTOGRAPHER

38.

38. COLOMBO CLASSIC YOGURT
COLOMBO YOGURT/CLIENT
PACKAGE DESIGN OF AMERICA/DESIGN FIRM
ALAN ANDERSON, GARY HOLDA,
 WALTER SOWINSKI/DESIGNERS

39.

39. CROQUI WHOLE OATS CEREAL

FEINKOST PRODUTOS ALIMENTICIOS LTDA/CLIENT

DIL CONSULTANTS IN DESIGN/DESIGN FIRM

DIL DESIGN TEAM/ART DIRECTOR

40. COUNTRY GROWN ORGANIC HOT CEREALS

COUNTRY GROWN/CLIENT

ASCENT COMMUNICATIONS/DESIGN FIRM

ALLEN HAEGER/ART DIRECTOR-DESIGNER

DARREL TANK/ILLUSTRATOR

LARRY STANLEY/PHOTOGRAPHER

40.

41.

41. DAIRYBROOK REDUCED CALORIE BUTTER

LEVER BROTHERS/CLIENT

KOLLBERG-JOHNSON ASSOC/DESIGN FIRM

GARY KOLLBERG/ART DIRECTOR

KOLLBERG-JOHNSON/DESIGNERS

42. CARLSBOURG

CORMAN/CLIENT

B.E.P. DESIGN GROUP/DESIGN FIRM

BRIGITTE EVRARD/ART DIRECTOR

O. SALLY/DESIGNER

JEAN-PIERRE DE SIMPELAERE/ILLUSTRATOR

42.

43.

43. SEA CHOICE PACKAGING

WASHINGTON FISH & OYSTER CO/CLIENT

TIM GIRVIN DESIGN INC/DESIGN FIRM

TIM GIRVIN/ART DIRECTOR

STEPHEN PANNONE/DESIGNER

BYRON GIN/ILLUSTRATOR

44. PROGRESSO SOUPS

PET INC/CLIENT

MOONINK COMMUNICATIONS/DESIGN FIRM

JOHN DOWNS/ART DIRECTOR

THOMAS JONES/DESIGNER

GEORG BOSEK/PHOTOGRAPHER

44.

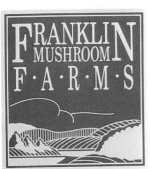

45.

45. FRANKLIN MUSHROOM FARMS

FRANKLIN MUSHROOM FARMS/CLIENT

CLIFFORD SELBERT DESIGN INC/DESIGN FIRM

CLIFFORD SELBERT/ART DIRECTOR

MELANIE LOWE/DESIGNER

MARK FISHER/ILLUSTRATOR

46. FRENCH'S SPICE LINE

DURKEE FRENCH CO/CLIENT

COLEMAN LIPUMA SEGAL & MORRILL INC/
 DESIGN FIRM

SAL V. LIPUMA, ABE SEGAL/CREATIVE DIRECTORS

WILLIAM LEE, JOHN RUTIG, LORRAINE FIERRO/
 DESIGNERS

J.C. CHOU/ILLUSTRATOR

46.

47.

47. CROWN HILL GRAPES

CARDINAL DISTRIBUTING CO/CLIENT

MARK PALMER DESIGN CO/DESIGN FIRM

MARK PALMER/ART DIRECTOR-DESIGNER

CURTIS PALMER/COMPUTER PRODUCTION

48.

48. AMAZING COACHELLA ONION BOX
CARDINAL DISTRIBUTING CO/CLIENT
MARK PALMER DESIGN CO/DESIGN FIRM
MARK PALMER/ART DIRECTOR-DESIGNER
CURTIS PALMER/COMPUTER PRODUCTION

49. AUSSIE PIE LABEL
FOUR 'N' TWENTY/CLIENT
THARP DID IT/DESIGN FIRM
RICK THARP/ART DIRECTOR
RICK THARP, KAREN NOMURA/DESIGNERS
SUSAN JAEKEL, RICK THARP/ILLUSTRATORS

49.

50. CHICAGO PICKLES
VIENNA BEEF CO/CLIENT
MICHAEL STANARD INC/DESIGN FIRM
MICHAEL STANARD/ART DIRECTOR
ANN WERNER/DESIGNER

50.

51. BURGER KID

SOGLOWEK-TEVA/CLIENT

VARDIMON DESIGN/DESIGN FIRM

YAROM VARDIMON/ART DIRECTOR-DESIGNER-
 ILLUSTRATOR

51.

52. SAUCE JOSEPH

NIELS BROTHERS/CLIENT

B.E.P. DESIGN GROUP/DESIGN FIRM

BRIGITTE EVRARD/ART DIRECTOR

CAROLE PURNELLE/DESIGNER

53. EDEN ORGANIC SAUERKRAUT

EDEN FOODS INC/CLIENT

PERICH + PARTNERS/DESIGN FIRM

ERNIE PERICH/ART DIRECTOR

JANINE H. THIELK/DESIGNER

DAVE SCHWEITZER/ILLUSTRATOR

52.

53.

54.

FOODS

54A.

54. WISHBONE SALAD DRESSINGS

54A. PRITIKIN

THE QUAKER OATS COMPANY/CLIENT

COLEMAN, LIPUMA, SEGAL, MORRILL, INC/
 DESIGN FIRM

OWEN W. COLEMAN, EDWARD MORRILL, ABE
 SEGAL/CREATIVE DIRECTORS

EDWARD MORRILL, WILLIAM LEE, SARAH
 ALLEN/DESIGNERS

RUDY MULLER STUDIO, EDMUND GOLDSPINK
 STUDIO/PHOTOGRAPHERS

55. YOUNG'S COD FILLETS

YOUNG'S CHILLED FISH/CLIENT

ELMWOOD/DESIGN FIRM

JULIA WHITE/ART DIRECTOR-DESIGNER

HEATHER BROWN/PHOTOGRAPHER

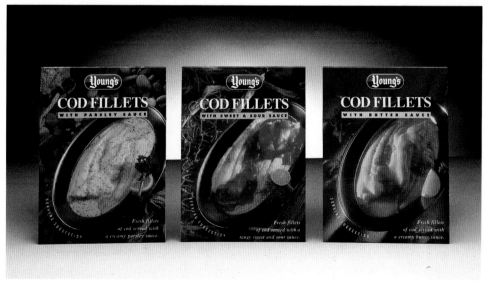

55.

56.

56. EDEN'S NATURAL SYNERGY
SOUTH CHINA ISLAND UNION/CLIENT
ALAN CHAN DESIGN CO/DESIGN FIRM
ALAN CHAN/ART DIRECTOR
ALAN CHAN, CHEN SHUN TSOI, PETER LO/DESIGNERS
PETER LO/ILLUSTRATOR
JEN HALIM/PHOTOGRAPHER

57. STOCKPOT SOUPS

STOCKPOT SOUPS/CLIENT

TIM GIRVIN DESIGN INC/DESIGN FIRM

TIM GIRVIN/ART DIRECTOR

STEPHEN PANNONE/DESIGNER-ILLUSTRATOR

57.

58. STOCKPOT SAUCES

STOCKPOT SOUPS/CLIENT

TIM GIRVIN DESIGN INC/DESIGN FIRM

TIM GIRVIN/ART DIRECTOR

STEPHEN PANNONE/DESIGNER

LAURIE VETTE/ILLUSTRATOR

58.

59.

59. SORRENTI FARMS

SORRENTI FARMS/CLIENT

PAGE DESIGN INC/DESIGN FIRM

PAUL PAGE/ART DIRECTOR-DESIGNER

JONATHAN WEAST/ILLUSTRATOR

60.

60. ZIZ NATURAL CHEESE SPREAD

KRAFT GENERAL FOODS/CLIENT

B.E.P. DESIGN GROUP/DESIGN FIRM

BRIGITTE EVRARD/ART DIRECTOR

NEVIN ARIG/DESIGNER

TRIAS/ILLUSTRATOR

61.

61. MASCIO'S PRODUCT LINE

MASCIO'S ITALIAN SPECIALTY FOODS/CLIENT

TIM GIRVIN DESIGN INC/DESIGN FIRM

TIM GIRVIN/ART DIRECTOR

LAURIE VETTE/DESIGNER-ILLUSTRATOR

62.

62. KUNER'S SOUTHWEST LINE

FARIBAULT FOODS/CLIENT

HILLIS MACKEY & CO INC/DESIGN FIRM

TOM ROPER/ART DIRECTOR

CHRIS SCHMID/DESIGNER

STUDIO WEST, DEL ERICKSON/ILLUSTRATOR

TODD AP JONES/LETTERING

MATRE RAJTAR, TOM MATRE/PHOTOGRAPHY

63.

63. LORRAINE LITES

STELLA CHEESE CO INC/CLIENT

LIPSON-ALPORT-GLASS & ASSOC/DESIGN FIRM

64. PILLSBURY BAKE-OFF

THE PILLSBURY COMPANY/CLIENT

HILLIS MACKEY & CO INC/DESIGN FIRM

TERRY MACKEY/ART DIRECTOR

TERRY MACKEY, EMILY OBERG/DESIGNERS

DAVID OLMSTEAD/ILLUSTRATOR

TODD AP JONES/LETTERING

64.

65.

65. EDEN ORGANIC TOMATOES & SPAGHETTI SAUCE

EDEN FOODS INC/CLIENT

PERICH + PARTNERS/DESIGN FIRM

ERNIE PERICH/ART DIRECTOR

JANINE H. THIELK/DESIGNER

DAVE SCHWEITZER/ILLUSTRATOR

66.

66. DIGIORNO FRESH PASTAS & SAUCES

KRAFT INC/CLIENT

MURRIE, WHITE, DRUMMOND, LIENHART/

 DESIGN FIRM

KATE MCSHERRY/ART DIRECTOR-DESIGNER

QUANG HO/ILLUSTRATOR

PAUL RUNG/PHOTOGRAPHER

67. PIZZA GALLEY

NAVY EXCHANGE/CLIENT

THE BERNI COMPANY/DESIGN FIRM

MARK ECKSTEIN/ART DIRECTOR

JUNG KIM/DESIGNER

67.

68.

68. LIRA OILS

MOLINAS RIO DE LA PLATA/CLIENT

AVALOS & BOURSE/DESIGN FIRM

CARLOS AVALOS/ART DIRECTOR

ELVIO SANCHEZ, CARLOS AVALOS/DESIGNERS

HORACIO VAZQUEZ/ILLUSTRATOR

69.

69. TUCKER GOURMET PRODUCTS

TUCKER FARM/CLIENT

RICK EIBER DESIGN (RED)/DESIGN FIRM

RICK EIBER/ART DIRECTOR-DESIGNER

JOHN FORTUNE/ILLUSTRATOR

70. KRAFT GENERAL FOODS PRODUCT LINE
KRAFT GENERAL FOODS/CLIENT
PETERSON & BLYTH ASSOCIATES/DESIGN F
RONALD PETERSON/ART DIRECTOR
JACQUIE FAUTER-MACCONNELL/DESIGNER
ROBERT EVANS/ILLUSTRATOR

70.

71. SPRINGTREE MAPLE SYRUP
SPRINGTREE CORP/CLIENT
KOLLBERG-JOHNSON ASSOC/DESIGN FIRM
GARY KOLLBERG/ART DIRECTOR-DESIGNER
KEN THOMPSON/ILLUSTRATOR

71.

72. DELICOTAGE COTTAGE CHEESE

NITZAN DIARIES/CLIENT

STUDIO KALDERON/DESIGN FIRM

ASHER KALDERON/ART DIRECTOR-DESIGNER

72.

73. SCHORR'S

HEBREW NATIONAL/CLIENT

PACKAGE DESIGN OF AMERICA/DESIGN FIRM

ALAN ANDERSON, GARY HOLDA,

WALTER SOWINSKI/DESIGNERS

73.

FOODS

74. TINA'S BURRITOS
CAMINO REAL FOODS/CLIENT
SMIMOKOCHI-REEVES/DESIGN FIRM
MAMORU SHIMOKOCHI, ANNE REEVES/
 ART DIRECTORS
MAMORU SHIMOKOCHI, NOBUO HIRANO/
 DESIGNERS

74.

75. OCEAN SPRAY CRANBERRIES
OCEAN SPRAY/CLIENT
KOLLBERG-JOHNSON ASSOCIATES/DESIGN FIRM
PENNY JOHNSON/ART DIRECTOR-DESIGNER
LYNN ST. JOHN/PHOTOGRAPHER

75.

76. SPRINGBROOK FARMS
BIL MAR FOODS/CLIENT
SHANNON DESIGN ASSOC/DESIGN FIRM
AMY LEPPERT/ART DIRECTOR-DESIGNER

76.

77.

78.

77. SARA LEE PREMIUM DELI

78. MR. TURKEY

BIL MAR FOODS, SARA LEE/CLIENT

SHANNON DESIGN ASSOC/DESIGN FIRM

AMY LEPPERT/ART DIRECTOR-DESIGNER

Index

DESIGN FIRM ADDRESSES

ABC Design
854 West 181 Street #8D
New York, NY 10033

Ade Skunta & Co., Inc.
700 West St. Clair Avenue
Suite 318
Cleveland, OH 44113

Advance Design Center
2501 Oaklawn Avenue
Dallas, TX 75215

Akagi Design
632 Commercial Street
San Francisco, CA 94111

Alan Chan Design Co.
201-3, 2F Shiu Lam Bldg.
23 Luard Road
Wanchai HONG KONG

Alternatives
236 West 27th Street
New York, NY 10001

Apple Designsource
311 East 46th Street
New York, NY 10017

Ascent Communications
724 West Lewis Street
Livingston, MT 59047

Avalos & Bourse Communicacion Visual
Florida 671 2' P 205
Buenos Aires 1005 ARGENTINA

BEP Design Group
Rue des Mimosas 44
B-1030 Brussels BELGIUM

Belyea Design
1809 Seventh #305
Seattle, WA 98101

The Berni Company
666 Steamboat Road
Greenwich, CT 06830

Broom & Broom Inc.
99 Green Street #200
San Francisco, CA 94111

Busha; Boston
79 Kirkland Street
Cambridge, MA 02138

Clark Keller Inc.
1160 Spa Road
Annapolis, MD 21403

Peterson & Blyth Associates
216 East 45th Street
New York, NY 10017

Porter/Matjasich & Associates
154 West Hubbard
Suite 504
Chicago, IL 60610

Puccinelli Design
114 East De La Guerra Street
Studio #5
Santa Barbara, CA 93101

Rick Eiber Design (RED)
4649 Sunnyside North #242
Seattle, WA 98103

Sally Johns Design Studio
1040 Washington Street
PO Box 10833
Raleigh, NC 27605

Samenwerkende Ontwerpers bv
Herengracht 160
1016 BN Amsterdam NETHERLANDS

Shannon Design Associates
355 Settlers Road
Holland, MI 49423

Shimokochi/Reeves Design
4465 Wilshire Blvd. #100
Los Angeles, CA 90010

Sommese Design
481 Glenn Road
State College, PA 16803

Studio Kalderon
12 Karlibach Street
PO Box 24070
Tel Aviv 69701 ISRAEL

Susan Meshberg Graphic Design
1123 Broadway #716
New York, NY 10010

Tharp Did It
50 University Avenue
Suite 21
Los Gatos, CA 95030

Tim Girvin Design, Inc.
1601 2nd Avenue
Suite 500
Seattle, WA 98101

Trickett & Webb
The Factory
84 Marchmont Street
London WC1N 1HE ENGLAND

Vardimon Design
87 Shlomo Hamelech Street
Tel Aviv 64512 ISRAEL

Wallace Church Associates
330 East 48th Street
3rd Floor
New York, NY 10017

Walter McCord Graphic Design
2014 Cherokee Parkway
Louisville, KY 40204

Weller Institute For The Cure of Design
PO Box 726
3091 West Fawn Drive
Park City, UT 84060

William Homan Design
1316 West 73rd Street
Richfield, MN 55423

Yestra Graphic Design
Merwekade 77
3301 AC Dordrecht HOLLAND